INDIA'S AFGHAN MUDDLE

Also by Harsh V. Pant in HarperCollins

The China Syndrome: Grappling with an Uneasy Relationship (2010)

INDIA'S AFGHAN MUDDLE

A Lost Opportunity

HARSH V. PANT

HarperCollins *Publishers* India

First published in India in 2014 by
HarperCollins *Publishers* India

Copyright © Harsh V. Pant 2014

P-ISBN: 978-93-5136-212-8
E-ISBN: 978-93-5136-213-5

2 4 6 8 10 9 7 5 3 1

Harsh V. Pant asserts the moral right
to be identified as the author of this work.

HarperCollins *Publishers*
A-75, Sector 57, Noida, Uttar Pradesh 201301, India
77-85 Fulham Palace Road, London W6 8JB, United Kingdom
Hazelton Lanes, 55 Avenue Road, Suite 2900, Toronto, Ontario M5R 3L2
and 1995 Markham Road, Scarborough, Ontario M1B 5M8, Canada
25 Ryde Road, Pymble, Sydney, NSW 2073, Australia
31 View Road, Glenfield, Auckland 10, New Zealand
10 East 53rd Street, New York NY 10022, USA

Typeset in 10.5/14.5 Sabon by
R. Ajith Kumar

Printed and bound at
Thomson Press (India) Ltd

For
Vaidehi

Of all the horrid, hideous notes of woe,
Sadder than owl-songs or the midnight blast,
Is that portentous phrase, 'I told you so.'
Lord Byron

CONTENTS

PREFACE

'The past is never dead. It's not even past.'

—William Faulkner

THE RISE OF NARENDRA MODI to the office of Indian prime minister represents a decisive break from the politics of the past. As the new government took office under his prime ministership, one of the first decisions it took was of inviting the member states of the South Asian Association for Regional Cooperation (SAARC) for his swearing-in ceremony. The decision was a surprise but was widely viewed as a great move, underscoring the resolve of the new government to embed India firmly within the South Asian regional matrix. It also underlined that even though Modi's priorities would be largely domestic, foreign policy would continue to receive due attention. Modi also immediately set for himself a frenetic pace of international travel for the remainder of 2014, covering countries as diverse as Bhutan,

Japan, Brazil, Australia, Nepal and those in South-East Asia.

A focus on South Asia emerged as a central strand of the new government's foreign policy priorities. Modi visited Bhutan in June 2014 in what was his first trip abroad after being sworn in as the prime minister—not only because he wanted to develop strong economic linkages among India's neighbours but also to check Thimphu's gravitation towards Beijing. External Affairs Minister Sushma Swaraj visited Dhaka the same month, choosing Bangladesh for her first stand-alone foreign visit since assuming office. She hosted Sri Lankan foreign minister and followed it up with a visit to Nepal a month later. The fact that all of India's neighbours in South Asia and the wider Asian region reached out to Modi was a good start for the new government.

There were numerous challenges on the foreign policy front before the new government—ranging from managing the power transition in the Indo-Pacific region with the rapid rise of China to re-imagining the contours of a robust strategic partnership with the US. But one of the most immediate challenges arose from the decision of US President Barack Obama to completely withdraw his forces from Afghanistan by the end of 2016, starting 2014. It was hardly surprising then that in their first briefing for the new government in June 2014, Indian intelligence agencies highlighted the withdrawal of the North Atlantic Treaty Organization (NATO) forces from Afghanistan as one of the biggest challenges confronting Indian counter-terror strategy in the coming years, arguing that it would increase terrorism and extremists' infiltration attempts along the Pakistani border.[1]

Days before Pakistani Prime Minister Nawaz Sharif's

visit to attend Modi's oath-taking ceremony on 26 May, the Indian consulate in Herat, western Afghanistan, was attacked by militants belonging to the Laskhar-e-Taiba (LeT).[2] This was the eighth attack on Indian missions and mission personnel in Afghanistan, all of them executed by the Haqqani Network or the LeT in league with Pakistan's Inter-Services Intelligence (ISI).

There are clear dangers of the regional security situation unravelling as Western forces depart from South Asia. Afghanistan aside, even Pakistan's future is at stake, with violence now rampant in Pakistani cities in tandem with the growing strength of the Taliban insurgency. By striking a Faustian bargain with the Taliban, Pakistani military and intelligence services have created a force that is now attacking their own citizens. New Delhi will have to assert its role in ensuring regional stability.

Even as Indian security challenges intensify with the withdrawal of NATO forces from Afghanistan, the Modi government will have an opportunity to reshape the contours of India's Afghan policy at a time when Afghanistan is also undergoing political transition, providing new opportunities to both states. The year 2014 is likely to be Afghanistan's biggest watershed since 2001, the year the war on terror began. On the face of it, the stage is set for India—a regional power with global aspirations—to rise to the occasion and assert its role in the new regional dynamic. But presented with a golden opportunity, India has been found wanting in chalking out a coherent, assertive and proactive foreign policy vis-à-vis Afghanistan. The time has come for India to fight its own battles instead of leaning primarily on the US and continuing to impotently blame Pakistan. A state that wants to be respected as a global power cannot shirk its responsibilities in its own vicinity, no matter how challenging they may be at times. If India is not willing to do that, it will be best served by restraining its global ambitions.

India will have to demonstrate real leadership in Afghanistan if it wants to protect its vital interests and lay claim to the role of a regional security provider. But, for this, it will have to first understand how exactly it ended up in a position where its much-vaunted 'soft power' in Afghanistan has failed to yield any substantive foreign policy dividends. The following pages reveal an all-too-familiar tale of strategic diffidence and policy myopia. There is a need to learn from past experience and chart out a new trajectory for India in Afghanistan if an India-led South Asia is to take shape.

Harsh V. Pant
London
July 2014

CHAPTER 1

INTRODUCTION

'Balance of power in the South Asian region has shifted long back. India has advanced economically as well as militarily far more than Pakistan. But I don't understand why India is still in the early 1980s' mentality ... Don't make concessions to Pakistan. Enough of Gandhigiri now! You [Indians] are seriously accepting being slapped again and again in the face.'

—Haroun M. Mir, an aide to the late Ahmad Shah Massoud, Afghanistan's former defence minister, at a South Asian conference in New Delhi in March 2012

FINALLY, IT WAS LEFT TO Afghanistan to decide that enough was enough, and it did make clear in no uncertain terms what it wanted from India. What it wanted and badly needed was a robust security partnership with India that included supply of weapons and defence hardware. The pretence that India's 'soft power' engagement in Afghanistan was enough had to go, and Kabul took the bull by the horns.

Ahead of the visit of Afghan President Hamid Karzai to India in May 2013, Afghan ambassador to India Shaida M. Abdali made a very important intervention in a debate that had become sterile in New Delhi. 'It is critically important that the two countries ... talk about more substantive issues than training and other soft issues,' Abdali suggested. He went on to underline that India and Afghanistan 'are required to sit down and discuss the contours of our security and defence cooperation to ensure predictability, to ensure protection of common cause, which is self defence against any perceived threats to our two nations'[1].

This was an important intervention because it was a reminder to the Indian foreign policy establishment that the debate about Afghanistan was not merely a debate between various 'schools of thought' in India. It was a matter of life and death for ordinary Afghans, and they too had an important voice in deciding how India reorganized its Afghan policy in light of the impending departure of Western forces from Afghanistan starting in 2014 and the resulting security vacuum that was likely to ensue.

The debate on what sort of a security footprint India should have in Afghanistan has been going on for years in New Delhi, and there has been no urgency in coming up with a coherent response. Even when it is clear that the stakes for India in Afghanistan cannot be higher, the Indian foreign policy establishment has been content in merely suggesting that India's developmental role makes India an important player in Afghanistan.

The truth is that all the developmental investment that India has made, with India emerging as Afghanistan's fifth largest provider of development assistance and Afghanistan the second largest recipient of development assistance from India after Bhutan, will come to naught once Western forces leave Afghanistan, unless India makes it unequivocally clear that it intends to strongly protect and enhance its Afghan security interests even in the absence of a Western stronghold.[2] And that's what the Afghan ambassador was referring to when he argued that the Indian 'investment in security and defence sector in Afghanistan means the safety and security of India' and sought a security and defence cooperation that goes 'beyond the current trend of cooperation'.

Over the last decade, Indian policy, despite the nation's self-image as a rising regional and global power, has been unusually dependent on the actions of other actors. For the longest time, there was a widespread belief in the Indian policymaking community that the American presence in the region would continue and this would be enough to secure Indian interests. This was a strange position to take for a nation that otherwise has had no compunction about underlining its credentials as a non-aligned nation and about bemoaning the use of military power by the US. Former Prime Minister Manmohan Singh had been candid in requesting the US not to leave Afghanistan as he knew full well that stepping up India's security role in Afghanistan could mean political mayhem. But even if American and Indian interests converged in Afghanistan, as they did and continue to do, there was no excuse for not articulating an Indian response to the Afghan crisis. And as Western forces prepare to leave the region beginning in 2014, New Delhi is once more at a loss to respond to the new strategic environment. If the Indian security situation deteriorates post-2014, as most serious observers believe is very likely, New Delhi will only have itself to blame.

New Delhi needs to urgently put its own house in order. Indian policy towards Afghanistan has evolved in fits and starts over the last decade—first rapid economic engagement, followed by an equally rapid disengagement and then complete reliance on the American security umbrella. Part of it has been a function of the rapidly evolving ground realities in Afghanistan to which India has had to respond. But a large part of it has been India's own inability to articulate its vital interests in Afghanistan to its allies as well as its adversaries. There is an overarching lack of coherence in the Indian response as New Delhi seems to be perpetually on the defensive, first making Washington the sole pivot of its outreach to Kabul and then petulantly complaining about American unreliability. On the one hand, India has been signalling to the US that it views a long-term American presence in Afghanistan as integral to its regional security. On the other, it has been reaching out to Iran, which wants to see a full and complete US withdrawal from the region.

Even as India has signed a strategic partnership agreement with Afghanistan, promising to enhance its role in the Afghan security sector with a particular focus on the training of Afghan forces, it has at the same time been reducing its economic footprint in Afghanistan. As a result, New Delhi has not only complicated its own future options but it has also lost allies, who find it difficult to view India as a credible partner in the emerging strategic realities in Afghanistan. As Western forces prepare to leave Afghanistan, India stands at a crossroads where it remains keen on preserving its interests in Afghanistan but has refused to step up its role as a regional security provider. New Delhi needs to recognize that there are no short cuts to major power status. The Afghan ambassador did a great service by reminding New Delhi what's at stake in the unfolding great game in South Asia. The message was clear: India will either have to step up to the challenge or get ready to be forever marginalized in Afghanistan and beyond.

New Delhi has long viewed South Asia as India's exclusive sphere of influence and has sought to prevent the intervention of external powers in the affairs of the region. The notion of a Monroe Doctrine similar to the one proclaimed for the Western Hemisphere by the US, purporting to place the region off-limits to new European territorial acquisitions in the nineteenth century, was explored by Jawaharlal Nehru, India's first prime minister. In justifying the use of force to evict Portugal from Goa in 1961, Nehru underlined that 'any attempt by a foreign power to interfere in any way with India is a thing which India cannot tolerate, and which, subject to her strength, she will oppose'[3]. Henceforth, the security of its neighbouring states was considered to be intricately linked with India's own security and was deemed essential if India were to attain the status of a major global power.[4]

With India's rise in the global interstate hierarchy,

tensions have emerged between India's purported role on the world stage and demands of the challenges it faces in its own neighbourhood. South Asia is a difficult neighbourhood, and India's strategic periphery continues to witness perpetual turmoil and uncertainty. Instability in Pakistan, Afghanistan, Bangladesh, Nepal, Sri Lanka and Myanmar has inhibited India from realizing its dream of becoming a major global player. It has even stalled India's attempts at building interdependencies and enhancing connectivity. India is surrounded by several weak states that view New Delhi's hegemonic status in the region with suspicion.

The conundrum India faces is that, while it is seen as unresponsive to the concerns of its neighbours, any diplomatic aggressiveness on its part is also viewed with suspicion and often resentment. The structural position of India in the region makes it highly likely that Indian predominance will continue to be resented by its smaller neighbours even as instability nearby continues to have the potential of upsetting its own delicate political balance. However, a policy of 'splendid isolation' is not an option, and India's desire to emerge as a major global player will remain just that, a desire, unless it engages its immediate neighbourhood more meaningfully and emerges as a net provider of regional peace and stability. Even as India continues to struggle to deal with its neighbours, Afghanistan, since 2001, has allowed New Delhi an opportunity to underscore its role as a regional security provider. India has not made much use of it so far, and, with Western forces all set to pull out, New Delhi runs the risk of losing it once and for all.

THE WEST CHECKS OUT

For the US, the ground realities in Afghanistan had been turning from bad to worse, and there seemed to be no easy resolution in sight. Developments in recent years—for instance, the emergence of an Internet video showing three marines urinating on the corpses of Taliban fighters and the Quran burnings in January 2012, and the American soldier killing Afghan civilians in March 2012—managed to inflame Afghans to an unprecedented degree.[5] At the same time, after all the hype about negotiating with the Taliban, the pretence was gone by mid-2012 when the administration of US President Barack Obama conceded that it had failed in getting the group to the negotiating table and expected that any progress on the political front would take place only after 2014 when most of the Western forces would be out of Afghanistan.[6]

The whole logic behind Obama's 2009 surge was that a final push with additional 30,000 American troops would be able to set the terms of engagement with the adversary in Afghanistan. But the surge was long over and there were few results to show for it. The Obama administration weakened its own hand by explicitly linking the surge with a timetable for withdrawal in eighteen months. Once withdrawal was put on the table, there was little likelihood that the Taliban would be serious negotiating partners. The North Atlantic Treaty Organization (NATO), the intergovernmental Western military alliance whose forces were deployed in Afghanistan, also began openly talking of considering an earlier withdrawal because of the growing insider attacks that had taken the trust deficit between Western and Afghan forces to an all-time low.

Faced with growing public discontent with military expeditions abroad and steadily diminishing economic resources, the US was forced to re-evaluate its entire strategy towards Afghanistan. The Obama administration became so keen on leaving Afghanistan at any cost that it discounted the dangers of a renewed Afghan civil war by suggesting that the Al Qaeda threat was located elsewhere and the cost of continued presence in Afghanistan was unjustified. By pulling troops out of Afghanistan by the end of 2016, much as he had already done in Iraq, Obama would have ended America's involvement in two wars. Facing a drumbeat of criticism from his opponents, who said he had squandered America's global leadership and emboldened its foes in Syria and Russia as well as in China, he declared that while the US remained the only nation with the capacity to lead on the world stage, it would be a mistake to channel that power into unrestrained military adventures.

In his speech to United States Military Academy graduates in May 2014, he suggested that terrorism remained the most direct threat to American security, though the risks of a massive attack on the US from a centralized Al Qaeda have taken a back seat compared to more diffuse threats from an array of affiliate groups.[7] Yet, even as he prepared his nation for a new global role, US intelligence estimates warned that Al Qaeda had started to re-establish itself in Afghanistan.[8]

American allies have been even keener on a withdrawal from Afghanistan. British Prime Minister David Cameron visited Washington in May 2012 to underline with the US president that Afghan forces should take over the lead combat role in the country by mid-2013, earlier than planned. The two leaders acknowledged that Afghanistan would not have a 'perfect democracy' by 2014. But they envisaged 'leaving Afghanistan looking after its own security, not being a haven for terror, without the involvement of foreign troops'[9]. Cameron made it clear that he thought that the public 'want an endgame' to the war in Afghanistan. NATO Secretary General Anders Fogh Rasmussen also suggested that the withdrawal of Western forces from Afghanistan could come sooner than expected.[10] The US president repeatedly underlined that the United States, Britain and their NATO allies were committed to shifting to a support role in Afghanistan by 2014, and that this would be an important step in turning security control over to the Afghans by the end of that year.

As public pressure for a withdrawal intensified in Western nations, important changes took place in Western strategy towards Afghanistan.[11] The most significant of these was that the moment at which Afghan troops were expected to take what was called the 'lead combat role' was gradually speeded up. After long insisting that Afghanistan would begin the process of transition by the end of 2014, in February 2012 then US Secretary of Defence Leon Panetta suggested that he hoped the process would be complete by mid- to late-2013.[12] What this meant was that there would be a steady withdrawal of Western troops from the very beginning of 2013.

And then in May 2012 Washington and Kabul signed the strategic partnership agreement, which envisaged the Afghan security forces taking the lead in combat operations by the end of 2012 and most American troops leaving by the end of 2014. However, this would not include trainers, who would assist Afghan forces and a small contingent of troops with a specific mission to combat the Al Qaeda through counterterrorism operations.[13] This then led to the US and Afghanistan finally agreeing in October 2013, after several rounds of tense negotiations, on a draft deal that would keep some US forces in Afghanistan post 2014. This was aimed at providing a legal framework for continued US operations in Afghanistan after the NATO-led combat operations ended in 2014.[14] In May 2014, Obama finally declared that, assuming the Afghan government signed a basing agreement, the US would keep 9,800 troops in the country the following year for training and counterterrorism, with the US presence shrinking by half in 2015 and to zero by the time Obama leaves office in 2016.

This is being done with the full knowledge that the governance structures of Afghanistan are unlikely to survive the departure of Western forces. Despite the enthusiasm with which ordinary Afghans participated in the 2014 presidential elections, defying threats of violence from the Taliban, the post–Hamid Karzai political milieu is also unlikely to produce a national government capable of addressing myriad challenges facing the troubled nation. Disputes about the electoral process for the 2014 presidential elections underscore this point. The credibility of the elections came under a cloud with claims and counterclaims by the two main contenders, Abdullah Abdullah and Ashraf Ghani Ahmadzai, in the process eroding the authority of the office of the Afghan presidency. The delay in the Afghan voting results in July 2014 undermined hopes for a smooth transfer of power ahead of the withdrawal of Western forces and reinforced deep socio-political divisions in the country. The building of a viable Afghan National Army—the centrepiece of Western efforts—at the moment too faces problems with growing green-on-blue attacks (series of incidents in which seemingly rogue Afghan security forces turned their guns on their NATO counterparts), high rates of desertion and low rates of enlistment.[15] Afghan security forces are not ready in any sense to assume control of the country despite that fact that the US military has nearly met its growth target for them.[16]

All of this begs the question as to who will negotiate with the Taliban if at all the group shows an interest in talks. Pakistan continues with its old game of searching for the ever-elusive 'strategic depth' in Afghanistan and has so far not given any indication that it has an interest in evolving a regional framework to stabilize Afghanistan. The West has concluded that it has done what it was able to and no longer has either the will or the capability to sustain a long-term military presence in Afghanistan. Domestic economic issues are more significant at the moment, and geopolitical developments of greater long-term importance, such as the changing balance of power in the Indo-Pacific region, need to be dealt with. The Obama surge was the last attempt to shape political equilibrium in Afghanistan by using the military instrument. It turned out to be less effective partly because it was half-hearted and partly because the main problem turned out to be Pakistan which no one had any intention of tackling.

Not surprisingly, the fear of the return of the Taliban is haunting Afghanistan. Even senior Afghan government functionaries have started to prepare for such an eventuality. Afghan Minister for Water and Energy Mohammad Ismail Khan, in an attempt to protect his own flank, is seeking to create his own militias to combat Taliban fighters after the departure of Western troops.[17] As regional and factional leaders decide to rearm, the already fragile support for the Afghan government would be further undermined, increasing the possibility of another civil war. And after the rise of the Islamic State of Iraq and Syria (ISIS) in Iraq and the collapse of the Nouri al-Maliki government in Baghdad, fears have only increased that Afghanistan too could fall apart after the departure of Western forces.

INDIA SHIRKS

It is in this rapidly evolving geostrategic context that other regional powers, including India, need to reassess their policies vis-à-vis Afghanistan. This book examines the changing trajectory of Indian policy towards Afghanistan since 2001 and argues that New Delhi has been responding to a strategic environment shaped by other actors in the region. As the Western forces prepare to leave Afghanistan beginning in 2014, India stands at a crossroads as it remains keen on preserving its interests in Afghanistan. But by refusing to be proactive, New Delhi has lost the initiative, thereby doing some long-term damage to its vital interests. This despite the fact that there are many factors working in India's favour. Thanks to historical ties and cultural influence, India ranks as the ordinary Afghan's favourite foreign country. The US has also changed its stand vis-à-vis India and Afghanistan. Earlier, the US viewed Pakistan as central to its success in Afghanistan and so did not encourage Indian involvement. But now it is frustrated with Pakistani machinations and wants India to be proactive.

If India seizes the opportunity, it will help India get a foothold in Central Asia and reduce Pakistan's influence. As Western forces prepare to leave Afghanistan, more Indian aid and more training for Afghan troops can stabilize the Afghan government and destabilize the Taliban, which has been telling India to stay away and not give in to the US. In June 2012, India received some unusual praise from the Taliban. One of the world's most feared terror groups patted New Delhi on the back for resisting Washington's calls for greater involvement in Afghanistan. If there were ever a signal that India would do a world of good in the region, this was it, and New Delhi would be unwise to miss the opportunity.

Former US Secretary of Defence Leon Panetta was very vocal in his appreciation of Indian efforts in Afghanistan during a visit to New Delhi in June 2012. The Taliban too recognized India's potential. Delhi has poured in billions in aid and reconstruction, and commands great soft power in the country. Little wonder the Taliban is concerned. Insurgents can make ordinary Afghans lose faith in their government in Kabul, which is known to be corrupt, as well as doubt the sincerity of NATO troops who come from half the world away. But India continues to rank favourably among ordinary Afghans.

Equally important, terrorist groups see a new US–India

axis as working against them. As NATO forces move out,
Washington would like India to step up its role as a provider
of regional security. India too has signalled its long-term
commitment to stability in Afghanistan, but the differences
between the two sides were always in how to reach that end
state. The US viewed Pakistan as essential to succeeding in
Afghanistan, while India remained suspicious of Pakistan's
intentions—and Pakistan even more paranoid of India.
So Washington shied away from encouraging Delhi and
offending Islamabad. This was the ideal scenario for the
Taliban, since it was protected by Pakistan.

Gradually, however, the US changed its tone and reversed
its stand. Washington is so frustrated with Pakistan and
suddenly so appreciative of India that it's even willing to
countenance Delhi's ties with Tehran. Former Assistant
Secretary of State Robert Blake went on to acknowledge
in 2012 that the US 'understood' that India has 'important
interests' in Iran and that if it wanted to 'continue all the
important things that it is doing in Afghanistan, it must
have access to Iranian ports to get its equipment and other
supplies into Afghanistan because they cannot do so directly
overland through Pakistan'.[18]

This combination is the Taliban's worst nightmare. It was
no coincidence that Taliban's praise for New Delhi came right
after the third US–India Strategic Dialogue, which established
new consultative mechanisms between the two countries on
Afghanistan. But the Taliban know that the weakest link here
is, unfortunately, India. New Delhi has historically aimed to
be 'non-aligned' as far as superpower interests go, and the
Taliban is goading it to take this go-it-alone attitude. The

Taliban's statement called it 'totally illogical' for Indian policymakers to 'plunge their nation into a calamity just for the American pleasure'.

The Pentagon was quick to rebut any suggestions that India had declined to get involved in Afghanistan, but Americans have been concerned that New Delhi won't play ball. Besides the legacy of non-alignment, the United Progressive Alliance (UPA) government in New Delhi was rudderless in its second term. It was distracted by coalition politics at home as well as a sharp economic slowdown. Indian policymakers had little time to do some serious thinking about Afghanistan and the need to bolster New Delhi's credentials to emerge as a regional security provider. This was unfortunate, since a stepped-up role would have been an excellent riposte to those who had started doubting not only Delhi's partnership with Washington but also the reliability of India to assume responsibility in its own neighbourhood. Former US Secretary of State Hillary Clinton had noted that the strategic fundamentals of America's relationship with India had pushed 'the two countries' interests into closer convergence', but New Delhi forced a divergence by doing nothing on issues critical to both New Delhi and Washington.

This is also very ironic. There has been a persistent complaint in the corridors of power in New Delhi that the Obama administration sacrificed Indian interests at the altar of pleasing Pakistan, which further allowed Pakistan's proxies to destabilize Afghanistan. But even when Washington started making it clear that it viewed Pakistan as part of the problem and India as part of the solution, Delhi continued to dither. The evolving realities in Afghanistan present India with a historic chance. If it doesn't have the will to consolidate it, it will lose credibility not only with the US but also with ordinary Afghans, and also lose the chance to expand its sphere of influence, compromising its ambitions to be a regional and global power of any consequence.

Ever since the fall of the Taliban in 2001, India has tried to be active in Afghanistan and a broad-based interaction is taking place between the two states. This is also a time when Indian capabilities—political, economic, and military—have increased markedly and India has become increasingly ambitious in defining its foreign policy agenda. Rising powers seek to enhance their security by increasing their capabilities and their control over the external environment. As a rising power, India has also sought to make its presence felt by engaging with its extended neighbourhood and forging economic, military and institutional linkages. In many ways, Afghanistan has become emblematic of such an ambitious course that India seems to be charting in its foreign policy.

India has a range of interests in Afghanistan that it would like to preserve and enhance. Apart from countering Pakistan, these include containing Islamist extremism, using Afghanistan as a gateway to the energy-rich and strategically important Central Asian region, and asserting its regional predominance. Yet the most important goal for New Delhi remains one of ensuring that Pakistan does not regain its central role in Afghan state structures. The last time Pakistan dictated terms in Afghanistan was in the 1990s, and Indian security interests suffered to an unprecedented degree. But then India was a weaker state, marginal in the strategic equations of major global powers, and so could be easily ignored. Two decades later, India is widely viewed as a rising global power with many more cards to play in Afghanistan than before. Yet, as Afghanistan moves towards an endgame with all the attendant changes, India remains marginal to the emerging ground realities in Afghanistan. India's perpetually reactive foreign policy ensured that India, over the last decade, continued to react to the actions of other actors in Afghanistan without developing an autonomous posture. This will have serious consequences for Indian security once Western forces depart from Afghanistan.

This book first outlines India's core interests in Afghanistan. Subsequently, the changing trajectory of Indian foreign policy vis-à-vis Afghanistan over the last decade is delineated by underlining three distinct phases of India's response to the changing ground realities in Afghanistan as set up by other major actors, in particular the US and Pakistan. The book then moves to discuss the regional power configuration within which India has to respond to the Afghan challenge. Finally, the challenges facing Indian policy towards Afghanistan are delineated in the context of a changing US force posture towards the region.

CHAPTER 2

INDIAN INTERESTS IN AFGHANISTAN

'Afghanistan is passing through a critical phase as it transitions towards greater responsibility for its own security and governance and as NATO/ISAF forces move from a combat role to an advise, train and assist role. Success or failure of this transition process will impact security and stability for many years to come, not just in Afghanistan but also in Afghanistan's immediate neighbourhood—particularly in Central Asia and South Asia. For many of us who are Afghanistan's immediate neighbours, we have neither the luxury of a "withdrawal" or a "draw down" from the situation that prevails in that country today.'

—Ranjan Mathai, former Indian foreign secretary, in London in October 2012

AFGHANISTAN: A VERY BRIEF HISTORY[1]

AFGHANISTAN IS A LARGE LANDLOCKED country of imposing contrasts that covers some 6,50,000 sq. km, of which two-thirds are more than 5,000 feet above sea level and contain some of the tallest mountains in the world. Of the land that is below 5,000 feet, only 10 per cent is suitable for cultivation.[2] Living in this harsh country is a hardy and independent population that is derived from a mixture of Islamic tribes, which are often as diverse as they are obscure. They have sought to exist within what has historically been a weak state with a strong society, and, despite their apparent lack of conventional resources, have been able to defy invading armies for many centuries. Alexander, Genghis Khan and Tamerlane have all sought to conquer the region of Afghanistan with varying degrees of success. Indeed, such is the reputation of Afghanistan in defeating invaders that it has become received wisdom that Afghanistan is the 'graveyard of empires'. This reputation has been further enhanced by the more recent British and Soviet invasions of Afghanistan, both of which are perceived to have been abject failures.

Most sources begin the history of the territory that is now Afghanistan between the years 500 BC and 300 BC, developing through the reigns of the Iranian Achaemenid dynasty, Alexander the Great and the Seleucid dynasty. Although this is the date range in which historians commence stories of Afghanistan, archaeological evidence indicates that urban civilization began in the region between 3000 BC and 2000 BC. Afghanistan is certainly a land of crossroads, where there have been a variety of religions, cultural influences and governments.

Beginning in 500 BC, Alexander the Great and his successors, the Seleucids, influenced the area with Greek culture for hundreds of years. The region that is now Afghanistan was part of a massive empire over which Alexander once reigned. Competing regimes found areas such as Mesopotamia, Central Asia and India to be more valuable than the Afghani territory, leaving it more easily accessible to Seleucus I Nikator, Alexander's cavalry commander, who would be his heir and founder of the Seleucid dynasty. Seleucus proclaimed himself King of Persia, Syria and Bactria after taking over the region. Under his rule, Ionian Greeks were brought to the region to guard the Eastern frontier, and Greek culture gained ground.

Then Buddhism came to the region via the Mauryan Empire as Emperor Chandragupta Maurya defeated Seleucus. The empire reached southern Afghanistan and lasted there for 120 years, leaving a mark on the region by not only extending the Buddhist influence further but also by expanding the Achaemenid Royal Road, which linked Afghanistan to northern India, opening Afghanistan to cultural exchange and textile trade. Such developments in the evolving culture of Afghanistan accelerated greatly under Chandragupta's grandson Ashoka the Great, who, among other things, ordered the construction of Buddhist edicts in the eastern Afghanistan region.

Between 200 BC and AD 100, Afghanistan went through Indo-Greek, Parthian, Indo-Parthian, Yuezhi, and Indo-Scythian rule. Archaeological discoveries suggest that Indo-

Greek kings ruled with a combination of Greek and Indian languages as well as blended Greek, Hindu and Buddhist religious practices between 200 BC and 20 BC. Additionally, at its height in the first century AD, the Parthian Empire stretched into Afghanistan and dominated in the region for 500 years. This rule died out over time mainly on its own until the next dominating rule came about from a branch of the Yuezhi. The Yuezhi were originally a Central Asian tribe of nomads. This subdivision of the tribe sealed the fate of the Indo-Greek kingdoms, and shortly thereafter formed the Kushan Empire.

The Kushan Empire ruled strongly from 20 AD to 280 AD and also continued the legacy of Buddhist culture in Afghanistan. During the Kushan period in the first to third centuries, political, economic, religious and cultural contact between South Asia and Central Asia greatly accelerated. Archaeological excavations, art historical evidence, coins and inscriptions illuminate the direct connection between the establishment of the Kushan Empire and the development of long-distance trade, and the cultural linkages between the north-western Indian subcontinent and the silk trade routes.

From the third century AD, at the end of the Kushan Empire, until the seventh century, the region, though fragmented, remained under the general protection of the Iranian Sassanian Empire. The years of the Kushan decline from AD 235 to 284 have in fact come to be known as the Crisis of the Third Century. This crisis was a result of the slow disintegration of the Kushan Empire into small kingships while the Sassanians attained general reign amongst localized groups of power. The founder of the Sassanians, Ardashir, and his son and grandson, Shapur I and II respectively, expanded their rule into a regime known by many names such as the Indo-Sassanian, the Kushano-Sassanian and the Kushanshas. This Sassanian rule was defeated by the mid-fifth-century invasion of the Hephthalits, or Huna, a Turk tribe from Central Asia, although the region continued to be governed by strong local rulers despite a multiplicity of cultures.

Shortly thereafter, beginning around the seventh century AD, Afghanistan became subject to Islamic rule, which has lasted into the present. In AD 642, Arabs invaded the region, defeating the remaining Sassanian and Huna rule, giving way to Persian rule until the Turkic Ghaznavids invaded in AD 998. Rule of Afghanistan remained fragmented, however, with local rulers continuing to attempt to rule their own territories. For the first time in hundreds of years, fragmentation of rule ended temporarily in 1219 when Genghis Khan led the Mongol invasion into Afghanistan. But his rule did not last long, and local ruler competition began once again upon his death in 1227.

It was not until Tamerlane came to Afghanistan in 1381 that there was once again a distinct ruler. He and his descendants ruled Afghanistan until the early sixteenth century, when the region fell to the Mughals, who had themselves come to India from Turkey via Afghanistan. The Mughals ruled for two centuries until the death of their leader Nadir Shah in 1747. Thereafter, indigenous Pashtuns influenced the rule of Afghanistan, or rather nominally ruled, until 1978. It was during this period that modern Afghanistan is considered to have been founded, specifically by Ahmad

Shah Durrani, who was elected king by a tribal council after the death of Nadir Shah.

Within this period, keeping with tradition, Afghanistan saw great competition for sovereignty. In the nineteenth century took place what is now called the Great Game, with czarist Russia and the British Empire competing for supremacy in Central Asia. The British saw Afghanistan as a vital piece in the puzzle of securing their rule in India. As a consequence, the British interfered in the affairs of Afghanistan, leading to a range of Anglo-Afghan wars—the first in 1839 and the second in 1878. It was not until 1880 that an agreement was reached establishing the boundaries of modern-day Afghanistan. Under this, Britain would formally manage Afghanistan's foreign affairs, though Afghans could maintain autonomy.

Amanullah Khan became the leader of Afghanistan in 1919 and immediately attacked India in retaliation for British interference. He was not successful in obtaining any territorial part of India; however, he succeeded in gaining control over Afghanistan's foreign affairs. This seizure was finalized in the Treaty of Rawalpindi, which ended the third and final Anglo-Afghan war. This date of 1919, 19 August, remains significant in modern-day Afghanistan, where it is still celebrated as Independence Day.

The last monarch of Afghanistan, Mohammed Zahir Shah, came to power in 1933 and would rule until 1973. Under his rule, Afghanistan remained neutral during World War II, but his sovereignty was questioned. Additionally, due to the long-standing divisions among the Pashtun tribes, tensions rose with neighbouring Pakistan, forcing

Afghanistan to orient its foreign policy towards the Soviet Union as a reaction.

Though Zahir Shah helped make Afghanistan's first written constitution a reality in 1964, Mohammed Daoud Khan, who had served as prime minister, staged a coup in 1973, abolishing the monarchy as well as the constitution, and declared himself president of the Republic of Afghanistan. He too was not successful in his rule and was overthrown by the People's Democratic Party of Afghanistan (PDPA), a Marxist–Leninist party, killing much of his family along the way to power and taking control of the government in 1978.

The new communist government under the leadership of Nur Muhammad Taraki was ruthless and strict in the way it executed its plan to transform Afghanistan into a socialist state, launching a quarter-century of war for control of the country. In fact, anyone seen as a threat to the new state was killed. Taraki himself was killed by his deputy prime minister, Hafizullah Amin, who ruled for just over three months and was replaced by the Soviet Union in December 1979 with Babrak Karmal, the Afghan ambassador to Czechoslovakia, as the new president of Afghanistan. His survival was dependent upon Soviet assistance as the revolt against the communist rule spread and the Afghan army began to collapse. Brutal repression led to insurgency against the communist government spreading across the country and increasingly acquired an Islamic orientation as various loosely aligned opposition groups coalesced into a political bloc called the Islamic Unity of Afghanistan Mujahideen (those who engage in jihad). Not only did young men living in refugee camps in Pakistan join the mujahideen ranks but they were also joined by volunteers from across the Islamic world, especially from Arab nations.

Military cooperation between the Soviet Union and Afghanistan had begun in 1919 when the Soviets provided economic aid and arms for resistance to the British invasion. In May 1978, the Soviets sent 400 military advisors to Afghanistan to 'assist' the government. The 1978 Treaty of Friendship, Good Neighbourliness and Cooperation signed between the two countries provided a legal basis by which Taraki could request and receive further Soviet military support in the fight against the resistance movement. A battalion comprising armour and infantry arrived in June 1979 to guard the government in Kabul and secure the airfields of Bagram and Shindand. This was followed by an airborne battalion in July 1979, disguised as technical specialists, without their combat gear. Further requests for troops were made up to December 1979 but not granted as the Soviets began to think that while Amin was happy to request further military support from them, he ignored their advice and started to seek closer contact with the Iranians, Pakistanis and Americans, and looked at offering self-rule to the Afghan tribes. The armed forces were breaking up, and invasion appeared the only option left before the Soviets.

In early December 1979, the Soviet general staff planned a much larger commitment that eventually became known as the 40th Army. This formation consisted of two motorized rifle divisions bolstered by an airborne division, two additional motorized rifle regiments and an assault brigade. While the 40th Army was brought up to readiness for operations, a number of precursor activities took place in Afghanistan, including the disabling of the Afghan mechanized divisions and the securing of strategically important tunnels and airfields. Finally, the political decision to launch the invasion was made by the Soviet leader, Leonid Brezhnev, with his central staff present, in a meeting on 24 December 1979.

As long as the Soviet Union continued to support the PDPA government, a mujahideen victory was unlikely. However, from the mujahideen's perspective, in order to succeed, they didn't have to defeat the Soviets but merely outlast them. Although the financial cost of the Afghan intervention was limited, it did act as a steady drain on a faltering Soviet economy and did lead to a growing dissident movement.[3] A more significant factor in the decline of the Soviet economy was the dramatic deterioration of East–West relations as a result of the invasion of Afghanistan. Following the death of Konstantin Chernenko on 10 March 1985, Mikhail Gorbachev was appointed general secretary of the Communist Party of the Soviet Union. His assessment of the value of the conflict was clear when he pronounced that Afghanistan was a 'bleeding wound'[4]. However, he first gave the 40th Army one more chance to deliver. When this was not forthcoming and the prognosis remained poor, he took the decision to withdraw for several reasons.

First, the material cost was hurting an already fragile Soviet economy, but this was not a decisive factor as the cost of the conflict in Afghanistan was only a very small proportion of the total Soviet defence spending. Second, internal reforms had resulted in greater openness and public awareness of events in Afghanistan, which led to rising internal tension over the cost and legitimacy of the conflict. Third, and most important, improving relations with the West, and with it the Soviet economy, stood a far greater chance of success if they were no longer engaged in Afghanistan.[5] In an attempt to limit the damage to Soviet prestige, withdrawal was not completed until 15 February 1989. Continuing support was provided to the PDPA in order to allow a dignified withdrawal and a chance for the PDPA to remain in power. Between 1980 and 1986, it is estimated that the conflict in Afghanistan cost the Soviets $7 billion annually, with 15,000 Soviet soldiers dead and 35,000 wounded.[6] The Soviets suffered a humiliating defeat in Afghanistan because, once it had become clear that the means made available to pursue the political objectives were inadequate, they were unable or unwilling to modify their strategy.

Withdrawal of the Soviet Union meant the end of Soviet aid and of the government led by Mohammad Najibullah as well which had been in power since 1987. The Najibullah government collapsed in April 1992, leaving Kabul subject to civil war as the fractured parties that had stood against the PDPA regime and the Soviet occupation began fighting for control of territory. Despite efforts by the UN and some of the neighbouring countries to mediate, there was no agreement on a power-sharing settlement. The factional fighting largely took place along ethnic lines, and groups frequently targeted civilians from rival ethnic groups. In an effort to cease the factional violence, all major Afghan anti-Soviet resistance parties decided to agree upon a temporary government in 1992, giving the defence ministry to Ahmad Shah Massoud, a Tajik warlord, and the prime ministership to Gulbuddin Hekmatyar, leader of the Hezb-i-Islami party, who refused to accept the pact. As a result, warfare continued, and in a struggle between Massoud and Hekmatyar, instability reigned and thousands of civilians were slaughtered in the following three years. It was in this chaos that the Taliban emerged in the fall of 1994 under the leadership of Mullah Muhammad Omar and steadily gained power, reconfiguring regional politics, perhaps forever.

While Pakistan, along with Saudi Arabia and the United Arab Emirates, was the main supporter of the Taliban, India, along with Russia and Iran, threw its weight behind the Northern Alliance which included anti-Taliban Afghan leaders such as Ahmad Shah Massoud, Abdul Rashid Dostum, Mohammad Mohaqiq, Abdul Qadir, and Sayed Hussein Anwari. As a consequence, Pakistan's influence in Afghanistan peaked with the coming to power of the Taliban in 1996. It viewed the Taliban as a means of controlling Afghanistan and undercutting India's influence. Pakistan has long believed that it can gain 'strategic depth' vis-à-vis India by influencing the domestic politics of Afghanistan, something Islamabad felt it achieved during the 1980s and the 1990s.

But Pakistan's perceived gains of the two decades came under threat following the overthrow of the Taliban in 2001. After the 11 September 2001 terrorist attacks in the US carried out by the Al Qaeda, then Pakistani President Pervez Musharraf had to choose between support for the US-led invasion of Afghanistan and its 'war on terrorism' or isolation as a backer of radical Islamist extremism. He also had to prevent Pakistan's 'strategic encirclement' as a result of closer New Delhi–Kabul ties. He promptly signed Pakistan up as an ally of Washington. This committed Pakistan, at least rhetorically, to supporting efforts to stabilize Afghanistan and to strengthening the administration of President Hamid Karzai. In this broader context, India's role in post-2001 Afghanistan acquired a new salience.

INDIA'S GRADUALLY EXPANDING INTERESTS

Given that a politically and economically stable Afghanistan was viewed as a strategic priority, India saw the effort to help Afghanistan emerge from war, strife and privation as its responsibility as a regional power. Moreover, the consolidation of hard-won gains since the fall of the Taliban soon emerged as a strategic objective for Indian foreign policy. India has a range of interests in Afghanistan that it would like to preserve and enhance, and it is towards this end that it has tried to expend its diplomatic energy.

Countering Pakistan

To a great extent, India's approach towards Afghanistan has been a function of its Pakistan policy. It is important for India that Pakistan does not get a foothold in Afghanistan, and so India has historically attempted to prevent Pakistan from dominating Afghanistan. India would like to ensure that a fundamentalist regime of the Taliban variety does not take root again. Pakistan, on the other hand, has viewed Afghanistan as a good means of balancing out India's

predominance in South Asia.[7] Good India–Afghanistan ties
are seen by Pakistan as detrimental to its national security
interests as the two states flank the country. A friendly political
dispensation in Kabul is viewed by Pakistan as essential to
escaping the strategic dilemma of being caught between a
powerful adversary in India in the east and an irredentist
Afghanistan with claims on the Pashtun-dominated areas in
the west.[8] Given its Pashtun-ethnic linkage with Afghanistan,
Pakistan considers its role to be a privileged one in the affairs
of Afghanistan. Given these conflicting imperatives, both
India and Pakistan have tried to neutralize the influence of
each other in the affairs of Afghanistan. Both are stuck in
a classic security dilemma in so far as their policy towards
Afghanistan is concerned. Any measure by either Pakistan
or India to increase its own security causes the other to act
in response, thereby causing a deterioration of the overall
regional security environment.

Despite siding with the West in its 'war against terror',
considerable doubts emerged later about Islamabad's
capacity, and commitment, to crack down on militants.
Kabul remains deeply suspicious of Pakistan, on which
its security is largely dependent. Pakistan's Inter-Services
Intelligence (ISI) is linked to the resurgence of the Taliban,
whose leadership is thought to be operating from tribal
border regions. The rejuvenation of the Taliban does allow
the Pakistani military to underline the nation's role as a
front-line state in the war on terrorism, thereby securing
engagement from the US. Musharraf and his successors,
former President Asif Ali Zardari and Prime Minister Nawaz
Sharif, have been unable to dismantle the infrastructure that

has provided funding, training and arms for the Taliban, though the ISI has been brought under more direct control of the civilian government since 2001. The security problems in Afghanistan can be linked to the military's continuing position as the predominant force in Pakistan, an institution that has, since the 1990s, viewed the Taliban as a means of controlling Afghanistan and undercutting India's influence there.[9] Having focused exclusively on the Taliban, it is struggling to abandon it now, and the tendency in the higher echelons of the Pakistani government and military to turn a blind eye to jihadist violence if that violence is focused outwards on Afghanistan, Kashmir or other parts of India remains as potent as ever.

The costs of such a policy to the Pakistani polity and society are evident with the growing hold of the Taliban in Pakistan itself. Pakistanis themselves argue that 'the common belief in Pakistan is that Islam's radicalism is a problem only in FATA [Federally Administered Tribal Areas], and the madrassas are the only institutions serving as jihad factories. This is a serious misconception.' This mindset, it is suggested 'may eventually lead to Pakistan's demise as a nation-state'[10]. Until recently, the Islamist militant groups nurtured by Pakistan's military and intelligence apparatus were focused on external conflicts, especially the dispute over Kashmir, the Soviet occupation of Afghanistan during the 1980s and the presence of US-led forces in Afghanistan since the fall of the Taliban in late 2001. In the past few years, however, extremist groups along the Afghan border have turned inwards, spreading violence and religious fanaticism among the ethnic Pashtun populace in Pakistan's north-west.

The increasing occurrence of insurgent assaults against high-profile government and civilian targets in other regions of the country—especially in Punjab, the traditional home of Pakistan's armed forces—suggests that militancy has spun out of the government's control.

Kabul has repeatedly blamed Islamabad for a resurgence of the Taliban. The rhetoric intensified to a level where Karzai warned in 2008 that a failure to bring peace to Afghanistan would be disastrous for the whole region and accused Pakistan of trying to 'enslave' the Afghan people. He even threatened to send troops across the border into Pakistan to fight militant groups operating in border areas to attack Afghanistan.[11] The deterioration of relations also manifested itself in a dispute over suggestions from the Pakistani government in 2008 that it would seal its 2,430-km-long border with fences and mines. Afghanistan, which does not recognize the border, reacted strongly against the plan, arguing that it would divide families and would not end cross-border terrorism. Islamabad insisted that 30,00,000 Afghan refugees should return home as one way of preventing Pakistan from being used as a haven by extremists. Pakistan also suggested that drug traffickers from Afghanistan (which produces 90 per cent of the world's heroin supply) were using their influence to campaign against the border plan. As casualties mounted with the Taliban regaining lost ground, Pakistan's role came under scanner over activities ranging from helping to plot a prison break in Kandahar in 2011 to even aiding an assassination attempt against Karzai in 2008.[12]

Pakistan's frustration at the loss of political influence in Afghanistan after the ouster of the Taliban was compounded by the welcoming attitude of the Karzai government towards India. Karzai may not be deliberately crafting a Delhi–Kabul alliance against Islamabad but he certainly hoped to push Pakistan into taking his concerns seriously. In a sign of its growing influence in Afghanistan, India opened consulates in Herat, Mazar-e-Sharif, Kandahar and Jalalabad, in addition to its embassy in Kabul. Pakistan accused India's Kabul embassy of spreading anti-Pakistani propaganda and viewed the establishment of the consulates as a way for Delhi to improve intelligence gathering against it. Islamabad also remains wary of Afghanistan or India exerting influence on the restive populations in its border regions such as Baluchistan and the North-West Frontier Province (NWFP). It claims that much of the funding and arms for the Baluch tribal leaders, grouped under the umbrella of the Baluchistan Liberation Army, are funnelled through the Indian consulates in Jalalabad and Kandahar.

Pakistan worked hard to limit India's involvement in Afghanistan. It made transit rights to Afghanistan conditional upon a resolution of the Kashmir issue. By not allowing India transit rights to Afghanistan through its territory, it sought to leverage Afghanistan's reliance on the Karachi port as its only gateway to the world. But Kabul pushed back and used Iran and India to find an alternative route so as to reduce its historic dependence on Pakistan for transit trade. Though Pakistan failed to achieve its objectives in the economic realm, it was successful in limiting India's military involvement in Afghanistan. It did not even allow India to send to Kabul a few hundred military transport vehicles, which India had to ultimately route through Iran.[13]

Despite Pakistan's objections, however, Afghanistan sought Indian assistance in the defence sector. The Afghan Air Force's fleet of MiG 21 fighters and other defence equipment, mostly of the Russian and Soviet origin, was serviced by Indian technicians. India also played an important role in the reorganization of the Afghan National Army and hoped that it would help in the long-term evolution of Indo-Afghan military ties.[14] India had to station Indo-Tibetan Border Police (ITBP) commandos in Afghanistan for the protection of its personnel employed by the Border Roads Organization (BRO). This was the first time since independence that India had its military personnel deployed in Afghanistan, something that did not go down well with Pakistan.

But with the Taliban openly threatening Indians working in various projects in Afghanistan, and after the death of a few of its nationals, India was forced to take this measure as around 3,000 Indian nationals were engaged in infrastructure construction, capacity building and development projects in Afghanistan. Faced with a resurgent and resilient Taliban aided by Pakistan, India and Afghanistan also cooperated extensively on intelligence gathering. Afghan authorities repeatedly hinted at the role of Pakistan's ISI in various attacks on Indian installations in Afghanistan over the last few years which the Pakistani government was always quick to deny. The message of such attacks, though, seemed clear to India: it should get out of Afghanistan.

Despite the public pronouncements of the US government in support of Pakistan, the sharply rising Western casualty rates in Afghanistan generated scepticism in the West about

Pakistan's efforts to rein in the Taliban and encouraged a rethink about Pakistan's role in the global war on terror.[15] In a clear indication that the US was turning up the pressure on Pakistan to crack down in its tribal areas, former US Director of National Intelligence John Negroponte cautioned the US Congress in 2007 that Pakistan was a major source of Islamic extremism and Al Qaeda leaders had found a sanctuary in secure Pakistani hideouts. Moreover, according to him, the Taliban was back to rebuilding itself in Pakistan with full vigour.[16] This despite the fact that the West, sensitive to Pakistani concerns, had pressured India to scale down its diplomatic presence in Afghanistan. Moreover, the Obama administration had indicated that it considered Afghanistan as the central front in the 'war on terror' and wanted to make Pakistan accountable for ensuring security in the South Asian region as the turmoil in Afghanistan could not be contained without addressing the sources of support for extremism and terrorism in Pakistan.

Under pressure from the US, which got alarmed by the growing hold of radicals in Pakistan, the Pakistani military was forced to undertake major operations in the Swat Valley, an administrative district in the Khyber Pakhtunkhwa Province (formerly NWFP), located close to the Afghan–Pakistan border, in 2009 and claimed success in retaking the region from Taliban insurgents, who were extending their reach towards the heartland of the country with great speed. The Taliban mostly melted away without a major fight, only to return when the military withdrew or to fight elsewhere. Yet the reassertion of control over Swat, at least temporarily, denied the militants a haven they coveted inside Pakistan.

In its October 2009 push in South Waziristan—the southern part of the mountainous region of north-west Pakistan bordering Afghanistan—the military was not successful. It failed to kill or even capture even a single top Taliban commander and the plans to provide basic services remained mired in conflict and mutual suspicion between the military and the civilian government, raising serious doubts about the ability of the authorities to keep control over Swat and other areas over a long period of time.[17] In June 2014, after years of resisting external pressure and being taken aback by the assault on the Karachi airport earlier in the month, the Pakistani military launched another major operation, this time in North Waziristan. It not only pushed Tehreek-e-Taliban fighters across the border in Afghanistan but the operation started after allowing the Haqqani Network commanders to move to safer havens. These operations were more about destabilizing Afghanistan by pushing Pakistani militants across the border than about fighting the extremists.

The long-term struggle against the Taliban remains complicated, thereby endangering the future prospects of any regional cooperative endeavour in tackling security challenges. Moreover, Pakistan has made it clear that only Islamabad and Rawalpindi (the headquarters of the Pakistan army) can bring the Afghan Taliban into the political mainstream. It captured Mullah Abdul Ghani Baradar, a senior Taliban leader, in February 2010 to sabotage the United Nations' direct back-channel negotiations with his faction of the Taliban, as the Pakistani army wanted to retain its central role in mediation efforts at all costs.

While some have suggested that increasing trade and

transit between India and Pakistan can reduce their sense of political rivalry in Afghanistan, it is not clear if the two sides would be willing to give up their power struggle so easily.[18] After all, it was as far back as 1979 that India had proposed that India and Pakistan should cooperate on Afghanistan to stabilize the South Asian security environment but global political realities soon took over, with Pakistan emerging as a front-line state in the US-led struggle against Soviet expansionism and India gravitating towards the other side. Pakistan, which has long viewed itself as the ultimate arbiter of power in Afghanistan, is finding it difficult to reconcile itself to a situation where the balance of power seems to have shifted in favour of India. The Cold War may have ended in 1991 but the security dilemma between India and Pakistan continues, and this will continue to shape India's attitudes towards Afghanistan.

Containing Islamist Extremism

India's other major interest is to make sure that Islamist extremism remains under control in its neighbourhood. Its struggle against this is also closely intertwined with the rise of extremism in Pakistan and Afghanistan. Pakistan has long backed separatists in Jammu and Kashmir in the name of self-determination, and India has over the years been a victim of the radicalization of Islamist forces in Kashmir, which have been successful in expanding their network across India. Any breeding ground of radical Islamists under the aegis of Pakistan has a direct impact on the security of India, resulting in a rise in the infiltration of terrorists across borders as well as attacks. It is vital for both India and Afghanistan that the latter never again emerges as a safe haven for terrorism and extremism.

Ever since the withdrawal of the Soviet Union from Afghanistan, there has been a gradual growth of Salafists (a militant group of extremist Sunnis who believe themselves the only correct interpreters of the Quran and seek to convert all Muslims and to insure that its own fundamentalist version of Islam will dominate the world) around the globe. India has been no exception, with the movement making use of the nation's liberal environment to preach and operate a radical version of Islam to sections of the 170-million-strong Muslim populace at a time when they have been particularly vulnerable due to the rise of Hindu nationalism. The Salafist ideology has been nurtured in the ultra-conservative environs of Saudi Arabia and exported to the rest of the world ever since the boom in Saudi oil revenues in the 1970s.

The founder of the Saudi Kingdom, King Abd al-Aziz ibn Saud, based his rule on the Salafi doctrine, and this remains the ideology of Saudi Arabia.[19] A combination of factors in the 1970s made it possible for the Saudis to promote their radical version of Islam around the world. This included the hike in oil prices that provided the resources necessary to penetrate globally, the coming to power in Pakistan of General Zia-ul-Haq, who put his weight behind the Islamist political parties and their madrassas, and the Soviet invasion of Afghanistan in 1979, which brought thousands of volunteers into the country to fight the 'infidels'. By the time the Soviet Union withdrew from Afghanistan, there was an army of young radicals who had been converted to the cause of the jihadist movement.[20] An ideology of violence predicated on the distortion of Islamic tenets spread insidiously across the crescent from West Asia through Afghanistan–Pakistan and was remarkably successful in attracting converts.

A friendly Afghanistan where religious extremism continues to flourish is seen by Pakistan as essential to keeping up the pressure on India in Kashmir by providing a base where militants could be trained for fighting against the Indian forces. The mujahideen fighting in Kashmir have not only drawn inspiration from the Afghan resistance against the Soviets but also drawn resources and materiel support from Pakistan.[21] Kashmiri militants were among the thousands of 'volunteers' from various Islamic countries that participated in the war against the Soviet forces. They went back indoctrinated in a version of Islam that destined their victory over the 'infidels' as well as important knowledge of guerrilla warfare.[22] India rightly perceived that the victory of the mujahideen against the Soviet Union would fundamentally alter the direction of Islamic extremism as Afghanistan would end up playing a crucial role in the shaping of an Islamic geopolitics, sitting as it does astride the Islamic heartland involving South, Central and West Asia.

While India would like to ensure that Afghanistan does not become a springboard for terrorism directed against India once again, the resurgence of the Taliban and Pakistan's ambivalent approach towards this growing menace remains a major headache for India. In recent times, the pattern of medieval Islamist ideology challenging the writ of the state is more evident along the Pakistan–Afghanistan border, where the resurgence of the Taliban is manifest in myriad ways. The Taliban forces have attacked Indian nationals working in reconstruction and development projects in different parts of Afghanistan in an effort to intimidate the Indian government.

With the leadership of Al Qaeda and the Taliban operating from Baluchistan, the NWFP, and the Waziristan areas of Pakistan, these attacks can only be expected to increase, especially as they continue to enjoy Pakistan's tacit support due to its concerns about the growing Indian influence in Afghanistan. Despite his status as a Western ally in the 'war on terror', Musharraf refused to unequivocally renounce the terrorist option as far as Kashmir and Afghanistan were concerned and his successors have given no indications yet that they intend to change that policy.[23] There is significant evidence that training camps of various militant groups continue to operate in different parts of Pakistan. The terror strikes in Mumbai in November 2008 further confirmed Indian suspicions that sections of Pakistani political and military establishment have no interest in renouncing terrorism as an instrument of their foreign policy.

The political and military establishments in Pakistan are yet to clear the cobwebs in their minds—in thinking through, and operationalizing, a policy of no tolerance towards the jihadis.[24] As the operatives and partisans of Al Qaeda and the Taliban move about with ease and propagate their ideology even in those parts of Pakistan where the federal government exercises real control, these organizations face little difficulty in recruiting cadres or raising funds. The resurgence of the Taliban is being supported by Pakistan's intelligence agencies not only because they are under the spell of the forces of radical Islam but also because of their entrenched opinion that the jihadist movement allows them to assert greater influence on Pakistan's vulnerable western flank. Pakistan has yet to deliver meaningfully on its promise of reforming madrassas so that none of them can function as training schools for jihadis.

From the beginning of the US-led war on Al Qaeda and the Taliban, it has been clear that Islamabad would not be able to compartmentalize the jihadi groups. The strategy of keeping the Kashmir terrorist groups active while clamping down on outfits operating in Afghanistan was never going to work—for the simple reason that there was no question of those who believed they were fighting a holy war of terror accepting a diktat that they should cross only one national border or fight only one enemy.[25] India will be forced to respond more aggressively if the Islamist forces continue to gain momentum in and around Afghanistan because the last time similar developments took place, India had to pay a heavy price for its nonchalance.

Evidence is clear that the terrorists who attacked Mumbai got training in Pakistan and were members of the Lashkar-e-Taiba, a militant Islamist organization that operates from the tribal areas of Pakistan and has perpetrated a series of attacks on India. If the Pakistani security establishment was involved in these attacks, it underlines Pakistan's unwillingness to desist from using terror as an instrument of state policy. If, however, these attacks happened without the knowledge of the Pakistani establishment, it underlines the inability of the Pakistani government to control the groups that it created in the first place. The Mumbai attacks allowed India to once again underline to the world that it cannot expect to win in Afghanistan by ignoring Pakistan's eastern frontier. The objectives of terror groups operating in Afghanistan and India are similar, and unless a holistic view is taken of the region, neither will Afghanistan stabilize nor will India get respite from these constant attacks.

India tried to build diplomatic pressure on the US and the international community so that the Zardari government in Islamabad could be forced to take substantive verifiable actions against terror groups operating from their territories. India's case was couched in a language that underscored to the world that if collective pressure could be brought to bear on Islamabad, it would not only benefit India but the global community's efforts in stabilizing Afghanistan. India also started demanding a fundamental restructuring of Pakistan's security organizations, given their culpability in the mess that is unfolding in Afghanistan and in the continuing menace of terrorism confronting India. But it was soon clear that the West neither had the capability nor any real willingness to undertake the policies that India is demanding vis-à-vis Pakistan.

The Pakistani army has also been successful in rebuilding its image as the guarantor of the nation's security against the Taliban to some extent. When General Ashfaq Parvez Kayani succeeded Musharraf as the army chief at the end of 2007, the army had lost all credibility, and public anger against the military was at its peak. Among Kayani's first moves to retrieve lost ground was to reduce the visibility of the army in Pakistan's governance. Meanwhile, the Mumbai terror attacks, which saw the Pakistani establishment whip up fears of an imminent military strike by India, gave rise to the first positive vibes between the military and the people in a long time, with the public rallying behind the army preparations for what was viewed as an imminent war.

The Pakistani military and the civilian government have conveyed an impression that they are united in viewing the Taliban as the real threat to Pakistan and that it is important to mend relations with India. Yet, the terms of India–Pakistan dialogue soon reverted to the old days, and then President Zardari's earlier ideas about more trade, less Kashmir and no first use of nuclear weapons no longer enjoyed wide currency. The Pakistani discourse on engagement with India also sought to balance New Delhi's demand for action against the Mumbai terror attack perpetrators with the reciprocal demand that India must stop, as charged, funding and arming terrorists operating in Pakistan.

Public opinion wants the Pakistan government to act against extremism and militancy, but these twin menaces have come to be only and completely identified with the Taliban. Despite acknowledging at the very highest levels that militants and extremists were deliberately created and nurtured by the Pakistani security establishment for short-term tactical gains, there is little appetite for action against the jihadi groups that target India or Kashmir, even though these have radicalized entire towns and villages in the Punjab province.[26] The same trend continued when Nawaz Sharif took office in June 2013, and, despite initial euphoria, nothing much has been achieved. In such a context, it is unlikely that India will be able to have a positive view of domestic developments in Pakistan, and so any movement in India–Pakistan dialogue will remain tentative.

A Bridge to Central Asia

Afghanistan is also viewed as a gateway to the Central Asian region, where India hopes to expand its influence. Central Asia is crucial for India not only because of its oil and gas reserves that India wishes to tap for its energy security but also because other major powers such as the US, Russia and China have already started competing for influence in the region. The regional actors view Afghanistan as a potential source of instability even as their geopolitical rivalry remains a major cause of Afghanistan's troubles.[27]

India was forced to increase its military profile in Central Asia after the diplomatic humiliation it had to endure in 1999 when an Indian Airlines flight from Kathmandu was hijacked by Pakistan-backed terrorists to Kandahar in southern Afghanistan. India had to negotiate a deal with the Taliban that involved the release of the aircraft in exchange for three hardened terrorists held by India. India then decided to set up its first military base abroad in Farkhor in Tajikistan, close to the Afghan border, that was used to provide assistance to the Northern Alliance fighters and later to provide assistance to the post-Taliban government in Kabul.[28]

India has used Tajikistan as a base for ferrying humanitarian and reconstruction aid to Afghanistan. India's air facility in Ayni in Tajikistan represents a major element in India's effort to promote stability in Afghanistan and to enhance New Delhi's ability to contain Islamic terrorism both in South Asia and Central Asia. The Ayni project was completed in 2010 with the help of more than 150 Indian

Air Force (IAF) pilots who went to Dushanbe to execute the project. Some members of the IAF continue to maintain a low-key presence in Ayni in a rare instance of Indian military's presence outside the country without a United Nations mandate, though in 2010 the Tajik government officially made it clear that Russia was the only country likely to use the airbase in future.[29]

The Afghan leadership has also expressed an interest in acting as a 'land bridge' between India and Central Asia. India's interest in a Turkmenistan–Afghanistan–Pakistan–India gas pipeline is also predicated upon stability and security in Afghanistan. Moreover, India has to keep an eye on various other states that have started expanding their own influence in and around Afghanistan. In order to upgrade its ties with Central Asia, India in 2012 launched its 'Connect Central Asia' policy, which calls for intensified diplomatic engagement with the region through a multi-level approach entailing political, security, economic and cultural connections. Besides oil and gas, energy-hungry India is eyeing imports of uranium from both Kazakhstan and Uzbekistan.

Iran has also been increasing its influence in Afghanistan, using its oil money to realize its self-image as an ascendant regional power. Iran's strategy towards Afghanistan seems geared towards hastening the withdrawal of American forces, preventing the Taliban from gaining power, and trying to keep Afghanistan under Tehran's sway. It played a major role in restarting the post-Taliban political process in Afghanistan and has pledged $560 million in aid and loans to Afghanistan. But Iran's role in Afghanistan has become complicated. As its relations with the US became confrontational over its nuclear programme, intensified by the rhetoric of former President Mahmoud Ahmadinejad, there were some indications that certain sections of the Iranian military, especially the Revolutionary Guards, might be arming the Taliban so as to weaken the American military in Afghanistan. The coalition forces in Afghanistan captured some shipments of Iranian-made weapons that were being supplied to the Taliban.[30]

Historically, Iran has also competed with Pakistan for influence in Afghanistan. Iran has not taken kindly to Pakistan's close ties with the US and Saudi Arabia. It had also been suspicious about Pakistan's intentions in establishing and supporting a fundamentalist Sunni regime in Kabul. Shia–Sunni strife in Pakistan has also provoked Iran to provide clandestine support to its co-religionists, the Shias, in Pakistan. Though the illicit nuclear trading network of Abdul Qadir Khan, the Pakistani metallurgist who headed the Khan Research Laboratories and is considered the father of the Pakistani bomb, also helped Iran in its drive towards nuclear weaponization, Iran has not been very comfortable with the idea of Pakistan being the sole Islamic state with nuclear weapons.[31]

Pakistan remains concerned about deepening India–Iran ties and Afghanistan's gravitation towards such an axis.[32] There was also a perception shared by India and Iran that Pakistan's control of Afghanistan via the fundamentalist Taliban regime was not in the strategic interests of either state and was a threat to the regional stability of the entire region. As opposed to Pakistan, which promptly recognized the Taliban regime, India and Iran did not establish diplomatic contacts with the Taliban. India and Iran, together with Russia, were the main supporters of the anti-Taliban Northern Alliance that routed the hard-line Islamic regime with US help in Afghanistan in November 2001. India and Iran have signed an agreement to set up a joint working group on terrorism and security, the main purpose of which is to share intelligence on Al Qaeda activities in Afghanistan.

Both countries have a shared interest in a stable Afghanistan with a regime that not only is fully representative of the ethnic and cultural diversity of Afghanistan but also is capable of taking the country on the path of economic development and social stability, thereby enhancing the security of the entire region. India is cooperating with Iran in the development of a new port complex at Chabahar on the coast of Iran, which could become India's gateway to Afghanistan and Central Asia. There is also another project that involves linking the Chabahar port to the Iranian rail network that is also well connected to Central Asia and Europe. What is significant about these projects is that India's relations with Central Asia will no longer be hostage to Islamabad's policies.

As the geopolitical importance of Central Asia has increased, all the major powers have been keen to expand their influence in the region, and India is no exception. It shares many of the interests of other major powers such as the US, Russia and China vis-à-vis Central Asia, including access to Central Asian energy resources, controlling the spread of radical Islam, ensuring political stability, and strengthening of regional economies. But unlike China and Russia, its interests converge with those of the US in Central Asia, and some have even suggested that it is in the US's interests to have a greater Indian presence in Central Asia to counter growing Chinese or Russian involvement.[33] China and Russia are not only competing among themselves for influence in the region but are also trying to minimize US presence. The Shanghai Cooperation Organization (SCO) is seen by them as an instrument to control the expanding US influence in the region. The SCO has also been working towards increasing its profile in Afghanistan given the impact on regional security of the threats emanating from Afghanistan.

While Russia might be sympathetic to Indian concerns in Central Asia, China will be reluctant to see India emerge as a major player in the region. Given China's close ties with Pakistan, it would not be too pleased with growing Indian influence in Afghanistan and broader Central Asia. China has not engaged as meaningfully in a post-Taliban Afghanistan as it can, given its resource capabilities, and as it should, given that it faces a restive Uighur populace in Xinjiang. A radicalized Afghanistan is not in China's interests especially as some Uighurs were involved with the Taliban and the Al Qaeda. For India, Central Asia is crucial in so far as its strategic capabilities vis-à-vis China are concerned, and India's aggressive foreign policy in Central Asia is an attempt to outflank growing Chinese influence in South Asia. Some see India's attempt to build roads linking Afghanistan and Central Asia and Iranian ports as a response to China's building of a deep-water port in Gwadar as a gateway to global markets for Central Asian resources.[34]

The Obama administration's decision to raise the level of political consultation with Beijing on its 'Af–Pak' strategy so as to be able to mobilize Chinese commercial and political strengths in the region to stabilize the region posed problems for India not because of a larger Chinese involvement in Afghanistan per se but because of the possibility that Beijing might try to undercut Indian influence in Central Asia and Afghanistan due to its special ties with Islamabad. However, while coordinating with the US in Afghanistan, India also intends to maintain cooperation with its traditional allies in the region such as Russia and Iran. India is trying to revive trilateral cooperation with Russia and Iran, hoping to develop a countervailing force to the Pakistan-based Taliban and Pashtun leadership. This will force some tough diplomatic choices on India as US–Iran ties get tense and competition increases between Russia and the US to increase their influence in the region in the coming years.

The Obama administration's decision to take Russian help in Afghanistan was, therefore, a welcome development from India's standpoint. Russia has agreed to open its airspace for the transport of American troops and supplies into Afghanistan—which has been acknowledged by the US as a substantial contribution to American efforts at building a new international coalition to stabilize the Af–Pak region. Indian interests are best served if the US and Russia work together to stabilize the region, and so the US attempt to decrease its near-complete logistical dependence on Pakistan by diversifying was welcomed by India.

Expanding Regional Influence

Another factor behind India's post-2001 Afghanistan agenda

has been India's attempt to carve out for itself a greater role in regional affairs, more in consonance with its rising economic and military profile. India wants to establish its credentials as a major power in the region that is willing to take responsibility for ensuring stability around its periphery. By emerging as a major donor for Afghanistan, India has been trying to project itself as a significant economic power that can provide necessary aid to the needy states in its neighbourhood. Moreover, India's long-term ambition to emerge as a 'great power' will be assessed by the international community in terms of its strategic capacity to deal with the instability in its own backyard.

America's 'war on terror'—its strategic priority since 2001—had at its centre the goal of achieving Afghanistan's stabilization. No doubt, India's interests were best served in helping the US achieve that aim. But it was also clear that India would have to make some difficult choices especially if the US's commitment to creating an enduring environment in Afghanistan waned and it left before achieving its long-term objectives. India will find the going tough if the US decides to revert to its policy of the 1990s, when, despite convergent security interests, it failed to develop an effective counterterrorism partnership with India.[35] Some have explained the US policy of continuing to tolerate Pakistan's complicity with the Taliban by virtue of the fact that the US does not consider the surviving elements of the Taliban as a threat to its homeland but just a menace to the peace and stability of Afghanistan.[36] And as the US hesitated in putting pressure on Pakistan adequately so as to force it to take a more responsible stand vis-à-vis Afghanistan, pressure grew in New Delhi to take a more independent approach that relies less on the US.

The Af–Pak strategy unveiled by the Obama administration in 2009 did not go down well in New Delhi. Describing the situation as 'increasingly perilous', Obama announced plans to send an additional 30,000 troops, bringing the US deployment to more than 60,000, and to increase economic aid to Pakistan to $1.5 billion a year for five years. Progress was to be monitored with a series of benchmarks and metrics imposed on Pakistan, Afghanistan and US efforts. There would be no 'blank cheques' and Afghanistan and Pakistan would be expected to demonstrate their commitment by ramping up their governance and rooting out extremists. Obama underlined the reasons behind this risky and costly strategy by suggesting—much like his predecessor George W. Bush—that Al Qaeda continued to actively plan attacks on US homeland from its safe haven in Pakistan. And therefore, the US goal remained one of disrupting, dismantling and defeating Al Qaeda in Pakistan and Afghanistan and preventing its return to either country in the future. The US took the lead and marginalized NATO in its efforts to secure Afghanistan and Pakistan. It also tried to cast its net wider by incorporating regional states, most significantly Russia, China, Iran and India.[37]

This approach involved exploiting the fissures in the Taliban and negotiating with those elements who could be reconciled to the broader objective of supporting the Afghan government in some form. Obama argued that such a reconciliation in Afghanistan 'could be comparable' to the successful US effort to reconcile with Sunni militias in Iraq. But the idea that the Taliban could be divided into 'good' and 'bad' categories might look appealing to outsiders desperate to make an exit. For India, such an approach was clearly problematic. Those elements of the Taliban which might be willing to strike a deal with the West just to see the Western forces leave the region would haunt the security of India long after the forces have left. While the US may have no vital interest in determining who actually governs Afghanistan so long as the Afghan territory is not being used to launch attacks on US soil, India does, and it would be loath to see any form of Taliban gaining power in Kabul. The Taliban—good or bad—are opposed to India in fundamental ways. Taliban leader Jalaluddin Haqqani, for instance, was viewed by some in the West as a 'moderate' Taliban. Yet, Haqqani was said to be responsible for the bombing of the Indian embassy in Kabul in July 2008.[38]

Despite this, there was a growing convergence between India and the Obama administration in viewing Pakistan as the source of Afghanistan's insecurity and the suggestion that the world must act together to cure Islamabad of its political malaise. In recognizing that the borderlands between Pakistan and Afghanistan constitute the single most important threat to global peace and security, arguing that Islamabad is part of the problem rather than the solution, and asking India to join an international concert in managing the Af–Pak region, the US made some significant departures from the American policy towards South Asia since 11 September 2001. India, however, remained concerned about the lack of a fundamental change in the operational dynamic of the US strategy towards Pakistan as Obama continued to rely on the Pakistan army to deliver on American and international goals in Afghanistan. Moreover, the US seemed to have bought into the argument that Pakistan was unable to act against extremism and terrorism on its western borders because of the tensions with India on its eastern frontiers. India's problem with the new strategy was that the Obama administration seemed to have given the Pakistan army the perfect alibi for not complying with American demands for credible cooperation in the war against the Taliban and Al Qaeda. The consequence of abandoning the goal to establish a functioning Afghan state and a moderate Pakistan will be greater pressure on Indian security. The brunt of escalating terrorism would be borne by India, which has been described as 'the sponge that protects' the West.[39]

In theory, as outlined above, India has some significant interests to preserve in Afghanistan, and the changing regional dynamic post-2001 provided India with some precious and rare strategic space which could have been used to further Indian interests. Instead, New Delhi never really articulated a coherent policy. There were debates and there were discussions. There were the tantalizing glint of 'soft power' and the banal rhetoric of 'smart power'. And at the end of it all, India has been left with little real power in Afghanistan and no real ability to shape the future of its very important neighbour. New Delhi's enemies have been emboldened, its allies have been disheartened and its partners are left scratching their heads as to what India really wants in Afghanistan.

CHAPTER 3

INDIA AND AFGHANISTAN: AN EVER-SHIFTING LANDSCAPE SINCE 2001

'Menon said he may be a "minority of one", but he thought there was more potential for success in Afghanistan than most observers in India. The British were convinced the coalition [NATO] would lose because they lost three wars there, but others had been able to tame the country.'

—Former Indian National Security Advisor Shiv Shankar Menon, quoted by WikiLeaks as telling a US senator in 2010

BILATERAL TIES BETWEEN INDIA AND Afghanistan span over centuries, given Afghanistan's close links to the South Asian civilization historically. India has traditionally maintained strong cultural ties with Afghanistan, resulting in stable relations between the two states. Of course, imperial powers such as Great Britain and Russia used Afghanistan as a pawn in their 'great game' of colonization, and, given the contested boundary between British India and Afghanistan, the ties between the two remained frayed.[1] But after independence, as the problem of the Durand Line, the boundary running through the tribal lands between Afghanistan and British India that was established in the Hindu Kush in 1893, got transferred to Pakistan, India had no reason not to enjoy good ties with Afghanistan, especially given the adversarial nature of India–Pakistan relations.

The Cold War also forced the two states to assume roughly similar foreign policy postures. While India was one of the founding members of the Non-Aligned Movement, Afghanistan also tried to follow an independent foreign policy and, for some time at least, was able to effectively play one superpower against the other, thereby garnering economic assistance from both sides. But given America's close ties with Pakistan and Soviet Union's generosity in providing extensive military and economic aid, Afghanistan gradually fell into the Soviet orbit of influence, resulting in the Soviet invasion in 1979. The Non-Aligned Movement was divided on this issue, and India was one of the few nations to support the Soviet invasion and occupation of Afghanistan, thereby damaging severely its prestige and credibility in the international community.[2] Given India's antagonistic relations with Pakistan, India decided to support Pakistan's adversaries and ended up supporting whoever was in power in Kabul with Soviet support. This came to an abrupt end with the victory of Pakistan-based mujahideen in 1992.[3]

The chaos that resulted in Afghanistan following Soviet occupation and their ultimate withdrawal in 1989 had far-reaching implications for global politics as well as Indian foreign policy. As the Cold War ended in the early 1990s, India faced a plethora of challenges on economic and foreign policy fronts. It had little time or inclination to assess what was happening in Afghanistan, and so when the Taliban, spawned by the chaos and corruption that dominated post-Soviet Afghanistan, came to power in 1996, India was at a loss to evolve a coherent foreign policy response. India's ties with Afghanistan hit their nadir through the Taliban's seven-year rule when India continued to support the Northern Alliance by providing money and matériel.[4]

Ever since the fall of the Taliban in 2001, India has tried to engage Afghanistan in a broad-based interaction.[5] This was also a time when Indian capabilities—political, economic, and military—increased markedly, and India became increasingly ambitious in defining its foreign policy agenda.[6] In many ways, Afghanistan became emblematic of such an ambitious course that India seemed to be charting in its foreign policy since the end of the Cold War.

India's role in Afghanistan can be divided into three distinct phases (the first two discussed in this chapter and the third in the next) as it evolved in response to the changing ground realities in the country.

PHASE I: A 'SOFT' ENGAGEMENT

India's engagement with Afghanistan readily became multi-dimensional after the defeat of the Taliban and the installation of an Interim Authority in 2001. This was reflected in an immediate upgrade of Indian representation in Afghanistan from a liaison office to a full-fledged embassy in 2002. India actively participated in the 2001 Bonn Conference convened to choose the leader of an Afghan Interim Authority and was instrumental in the emergence of post-Taliban governing and political authority in Afghanistan. Since then, India's main focus has been to support the Afghan government and the political process in the country as mandated under the Bonn agreement of 2001.[7] It has continued to pursue a policy of high-level engagement with Afghanistan through extensive and wide-ranging humanitarian, financial and project assistance as well as participation in international efforts aimed at political reconciliation and economic rebuilding of Afghanistan. As the second largest recipient of Indian development assistance after Bhutan, Afghanistan stood out as a nation where New Delhi made substantive economic investment so as to secure its strategic interests (see tables on pages 58 and 64).

India's relations with Afghanistan steadily improved for a number of reasons. Unlike Pakistan, ties between India and Afghanistan are not hampered by the existence of a contiguous, and contested, border. Its support for the Northern Alliance against the Pakistan-backed Taliban in the 1990s strengthened its position in Kabul after 2001. Many members of the Alliance are members of the government or hold influential provincial posts. India has tried to restore the balance in its engagement with a range of different ethnic groups and political affiliations in Afghanistan. The balance was tilted towards the Tajik-dominated Northern Alliance during the 1990s as a counter to Pakistan-controlled hard-

India's growing 'soft power' in Afghanistan since 2001

Number of visits of the Indian prime minister to Afghanistan	Number of visits of the Afghan president to India	India's total bilateral aid to Afghanistan	Major infrastructure projects undertaken by India in Afghanistan	Major Indian companies in Afghanistan	Number of Afghan students in India
2 (11 May 2011; 28-29 August 2005)	8 (26 May 2014; 20-22 May 2013; 9 November 2012; 3 October 2011; 22 April 2010; 3-5 August 2008; 15-19 November 2006; 9-13 April 2006)	India has offered $1.2 billion for Afghanistan's reconstruction, making it the largest regional donor to the country. India has pledged just under $2 billion to Afghanistan, and spent around $1 billion, making it the fifth largest bilateral donor after the US, UK, Japan and Germany	Transmission line from Pul-e-Khumri to Kabul ($120 million) Afghan parliament in Kabul ($27 million) Salma Dam power project in Herat ($130 million) Zaranj-Delaram road ($150 million) Expansion of the national TV network	Approximately 100 Indian companies have invested in Afghanistan since 2001. The breakdown in investment by sector is 43 per cent in services, 41 per cent in construction and 16 per cent in industries. Some of the major companies include: Steel Authority of India Ltd, India's Afghan Iron & Steel Consortium, and ONGC Videsh Ltd	About 5,500 Afghan students are currently in India More than 100 Afghan officers are attending Indian military colleges

line Pashtun factions, led by the Taliban. India has used its vocal support for Karzai, an ethnic Pashtun educated in India, to demonstrate its keenness to revive its close ties with Pashtuns.

During each of the visits to India by Afghanistan's president, several important bilateral initiatives were announced by the two sides. These included a $150-million financial commitment by India for the construction of a 220-km Zaranj–Delaram road in the Nimruz province of Afghanistan; a preferential trade agreement between the two states; memoranda of understanding of cooperation in the fields of civil aviation, media and information, rural development, standardization, and education; and the establishment of a joint committee at the level of commerce ministers to conclude an EXIM Bank line of credit to the tune of $50 million to promote business-to-business relations. Afghanistan has also sought Indian aid in agri-technology, which would halt desertification, deforestation and water wastage.[8] Afghanistan was self-sufficient in food until the 1970s, but since then the vagaries of war, drought and mismanagement have wreaked havoc on the nation's agricultural system.

Former Indian Prime Minister Manmohan Singh visited Afghanistan in 2005, the first by an Indian head of government in twenty-nine years. Indira Gandhi was the last Indian prime minister to visit Kabul in 1976. In an act of significant symbolism, Singh's visit was also the first by a foreign head of state or government to last for more than a day since the ouster of the Taliban in 2001 as Singh brushed aside concerns about his security and demonstrated India's special commitment to Afghanistan. This visit was aimed at reaffirming the commitment of both sides to reinvigorate past ties and develop a new partnership as well as to mark the consolidation of traditional bonds, which were severed during the rule of the Taliban.

In consonance with the priorities laid down by the Afghanistan's government as outlined in the Afghanistan National Development Strategy, Indian assistance has focused on building human capital and physical infrastructure, improving security and helping the agricultural and other important sectors of the country's economy such as education, health, transport, telecommunications, civil aviation, irrigation, power generation, industry and rural development. In the realm of defence, India's support has been limited to supplying defensive military equipment such as armoured check posts and watchtowers to Afghanistan.

India and Afghanistan have a long-standing record of technical and economic cooperation in various fields as, prior to 1979, Afghanistan was the largest partner in India's technical and economic cooperation programme.[9] India launched an extensive assistance programme in Afghanistan immediately after the fall of the Taliban regime in 2001 and pledged $750 million towards reconstruction efforts, most of which was unconditional. Of this, more than $450 million has already been utilized, and the projects range from humanitarian and infrastructure to health and rural development and training of diplomats and bureaucrats. Delhi has emerged as one of Afghanistan's top six donors, having extended a $500-million aid package in 2001 and gradually increased it ever since.

Among the most high-profile of infrastructure projects undertaken by India was the reconstruction of the 220-km-long Zaranj–Delaram road at a cost of $150 million. The road will enable Afghanistan to have access to sea via Iran and will provide a shorter route for Indian goods to reach Afghanistan. This project was completed in 2008 by India's Border Roads Organization despite stiff resistance from the Taliban. Eleven Indians and 129 Afghans lost their lives during the completion of this project. The security of the Indian workers working on this project was provided by a 300-strong paramilitary force provided by India itself, because of which the project overshot time and monetary deadlines. After its success with the project, India has been asked to help in connecting Afghanistan to its other Central Asian neighbours like Turkmenistan and Tajikistan.[10]

India is also investing in the rebuilding of institutional capacity in Afghanistan by providing training to more than 700 Afghans in various professions, including diplomats, lawyers, judges, doctors, paramedics, women entrepreneurs, teachers, officials in various departments of Afghanistan's government, public officials and cartographers. Afghanistan's budding public transport system relies on Indian support as India not only provides buses but also training to traffic operators and other personnel related to transport. India gifted 400 buses to Afghanistan initially, followed by 200 mini-buses and 105 utility vehicles to lay the groundwork for a modern public transport system. India also gifted three airbus aircrafts to get Afghanistan's native carrier, Ariana Afghan Airlines, off the ground and continues to train airline officials to develop capacities in this crucial area. The new parliament building in Kabul, constructed with Indian help, is perhaps the most visible sign of India's outreach to Afghanistan as a fellow democracy. India's Bureau of Parliamentary Study and Training provides training to officials of the Afghan National Assembly Secretariat. India's Election Commission has signed a memorandum of understanding with its Afghan counterpart, leading to mutual visits and regular exchanges for training and study purposes.

India has been providing 500 short- and medium-term training slots annually to Afghan public servants and 500 scholarships to Afghan students for studying at the undergraduate and postgraduate levels. Around 5,500 Afghan students are studying in India as of June 2013, of which about 300 are women. Afghans want to come to India because of the low cost of living, scholarships, familiarity with Indian culture, good bilateral relations, easy-to-obtain visas and use of English in Indian educational institutions. Of the 2,325 scholarships given annually to international students by the Indian Council for Cultural Relations, 675 are reserved for Afghans, the largest for any nationality.[11] In July 2014, India liberalized its visa policy for Afghan citizens, allowing them to stay in India for up to two years and exempting police reporting for senior citizens and children.

India's commitment of 1 million tonne of wheat aid to Afghanistan has been operationalized, partly in the form of high-protein biscuits for school feeding programmes in Afghanistan through the channels of the World Food Programme. India is also funding and executing the Salma Dam Power Project in Herat province involving a commitment of around $80 million as well as the 202-km-long double circuit transmission line from Pul-e-Khumri to Kabul.[12] India agreed to adopt 100 villages in Afghanistan to promote rural development by introducing solar electrification and rainwater harvesting technologies. Five Indian medical missions have been operating in Kabul, Herat, Jalalabad, Kandahar and Mazar-e-Sharif, with nearly 3,60,000 poor patients using their services annually. India also worked towards the rehabilitation of the only hospital for children in Afghanistan—the Indira Gandhi Institute for Child Health—and has worked towards upgrading its capacity in various spheres.

India has a fundamental interest in ensuring that Afghanistan emerges as a stable and economically integrated state in the region. Though Afghanistan's economy has recovered significantly since the fall of the Taliban, with the real Gross Domestic Product (GDP) growth rate exceeding 12 per cent in 2012, it remains highly dependent on foreign aid and trade with neighbouring countries.[13] The only way in which any Afghan government can retain and enhance its legitimacy is by bringing the Afghan economy back on track. For this, it largely depends on other states, and India is playing an important role by laying the foundations for sustainable economic development in its neighbour. Bilateral trade between India and Afghanistan reached $600 million in 2011 and is expected to reach $1 billion by 2015. The preferential trade agreement signed by India and Afghanistan gives substantial duty concessions to certain categories of Afghan dry fruits when entering India, with Afghanistan allowing reciprocal concessions to Indian products such as

Humanitarian Assistance	Small and Community-based Development Projects	Education and Capacity Development
100g of high-protein biscuits daily to 2 million children under the School Feeding Programme (World Food Programme) Gift of 2,50,000 tonnes of wheat announced in January 2009 5 Indian medical missions give free medical consultation and medicines to 30,000 Afghans monthly Reconstruction of the Indira Gandhi Institute of Child Health in Kabul 400 buses, 200 mini-buses, 105 utility vehicles, 285 military vehicles for the Afghan National Army and 10 ambulances across 5 cities	84 small projects are under different stages of implementation in 19 provinces of Afghanistan Focus on local ownership and management Projects extend to agriculture, rural development, education, health, vocational training and solar energy	500 annual short-term Indian Technical and Economic Cooperation Training Programmes for Afghan public servants in Indian technical and professional institutions Reconstruction of Habibia School, Kabul 500 annual long-term university scholarships for undergraduate and postgraduate Afghans in India (sponsored by the Indian Council for Cultural Relations) 20 Indian civil servants given as coaches and mentors under the Capacity for the Afghan Public Service programme India–Afghanistan Vocational Training Centre in Kabul (carpentry, plumbing, welding, masonry, tailoring) by Confederation of Indian Industry Women's Vocational Training Centre in Bagh-e-Zanana (for war widows and orphans) by Indian NGO SEWA

Humanitarian Assistance	Small and Community-based Development Projects	Education and Capacity Development
5 toilet/sanitation complexes in Kabul		Capacity building programmes (diplomacy, media, civil aviation, agricultural research/ education, health care/ medicinal science, tourism, education, standardization, rural development, public administration, electoral management and administration and local governance

Source: *India and Afghanistan: A Development Partnership*, External Publicity Division, Ministry of External Affairs, Government of India, http://www.mea.gov.in/Uploads/PublicationDocs/176_india-and-afghanistan-a-development-partnership.pdf

sugar, tea and pharmaceuticals.

Bollywood remains immensely popular in Afghanistan, which was the biggest market for its films until the early 1990s. Even the ban on them imposed by the Taliban during their rule failed to make any substantive dent in their popularity. According to Sujeet Sarkar, an international advisor on governance, 'The common Afghan loves Bollywood films because they revolve around fighting injustice, which is omnipresent in contemporary society. This inevitably touches a raw nerve in them. The larger-than-life representations of the Bollywood heroes, in sharp contrast to their stark reality, provide them a vicarious opportunity to immerse themselves into the grandiose reel-life fantasies.'[14]

Ordinary Afghans have also lapped up Indian television soap operas and Hindi film music, underscoring not only the close cultural links between the two nations but also generating people-to-people affinity.

It was not surprising, therefore, when US diplomats asked India to send Bollywood stars to tour Afghanistan to help in global efforts to bring stability to the country. In a confidential March 2007 cable which addressed the need for 'specific, concrete ideas for opportunities for India to use soft power in helping Afghanistan's reconstruction', it was recommended that 'willing Indian celebrities could be asked to travel to Afghanistan to help bring attention to social issues there'.[15]

A VIGNETTE FROM AFGHANISTAN*

It was a lazy afternoon in April 2013, and Fridoon, whom I had met at a common friend's place a few days previously, had agreed to take me to the ruins of the Darul Aman palace in Kabul. He didn't have much to do as the plug had been pulled on the organization for which he was working. Left with little money, it had overnight laid off all of its employees just days before my arrival in the country. It was still easy for Fridoon as the organization was run by his sister, but that gave little reprieve to the rest. In any case, if the withdrawal of Western forces had not been on the cards, a trip to the palace on a Wednesday would have been a tad bit difficult. Now, I knew what to expect out of the ruins—Afghanistan is littered with such ruins and I had already been to a number of them—and also knew that I would spend little time there once I had expressed my regrets, cursed the war in general, taken some pictures and blamed the government for being corrupt and not fixing the ruins for which it had allotted a share of its trifling GDP. But the visit lasted longer than I expected.

A barbed wire fence and an army checkpoint guarded the ruins as if there was more left to be destroyed. The gardens around the palace, which is on a hillock about 15 km outside the Kabul city centre, were also in a shambles, barring a few small trees. Standing in front of the ruins, no one could say whether the palace was destroyed a couple of decades or a week previously. (The palace had been destroyed in the early 1990s after the fall of the Najibullah government.)

'Brother, the Russians built at least something for Afghanistan. The Americans will leave nothing behind. Maybe some tents and a few soldiers,' said Fridoon. 'The government has money to fix this, but it will not. It fears that if a civil war breaks out, it will be destroyed once again,' he added and walked away.

While I toyed with my camera, trying to find the right shell hole in the ruins to grace my Facebook photo album, Fridoon pointed to something behind. 'Look at that,' he said. 'The government will work from there once it is ready. I hope they view the palace every day and feel ashamed. Maybe then they will fix it. Who knows?' Just behind, there was a massive structure being built, with few workers but many big cranes. It was the new parliament building which India had gifted the Afghans. The sight was surreal and ironic—the clichéd symbol of democracy coming up against one of civil war.

Under a small tree that must have been planted not more than a few months ago sat a group of nine Afghan teenagers. One of them called out to me, 'Aye, Hindustani?

Aye! Salman Khan!' followed by a fit of laughter. Though it was part question and part statement, they had instinctively recognized my India connection.

I turned around and went up to them. 'Haan Hindustani hoon, Dilli se. Tu Kabul se hai? (Yes, I am Indian, from Delhi. Are you from Kabul?)' I responded.

'Haan, Kabul se. [Laughter] Tu Salman Khan se mila hai? (Yes, I'm from Kabul. Have you met Salman Khan?)' More laughter. 'Main Salman Khan ka fan hai, aur tum? (I am a Salman Khan fan. What about you?).'

This led to much hand-shaking and exchange of smiles and greetings. I also took a picture of the group with their permission and stood around for a while listening to them speak to each other in Dari. What I didn't realize was that the question on Salman Khan, a Bollywood star, was not casual. Speaking in Dari, they had reached a consensus—of which I was informed later by Fridoon—in all earnestness that Shah Rukh Khan, another rival star, did not match up.

'So, Salman Khan?' they asked again.

I said, 'Haan, Salman achcha hai (Yes, Salman is good) ... Shah Rukh?'

'Nai nai, Shah Rukh nahi (No, no, not Shah Rukh),' they said.

'Sanju baba!' said one of them laughing, referring to Sanjay Dutt, and showed his non-existent biceps. And then, almost immediately, almost naturally, he gave me his joint of hashish. 'Dost Hindustani, hashish Kandahari (Indian friend, here's hashish from Kandahar).' I held the joint, sat with them and took a long drag. Just like that, we had become friends.

---

* This was shared with me by a student of mine who went to Afghanistan to undertake research work for his Ph.D dissertation.

Kabul wants Indian businesses to take advantage of the low tax regime to help develop a manufacturing hub in areas such as cement, oil and gas, electricity, and in services including hotels, banking and communications. The Afghan government has been urging the Indian corporate sector to invest in Afghanistan and has even decided to accord special treatment to Indian investors.[16] A consortium of Indian steel companies, led by the National Mineral Development Corporation, India's largest iron ore miner, made a successful bid to acquire mining rights in Afghanistan's 1.8-billion-tonne Hajigak iron ore mines.[17] This bid is a rare instance of public and private sector companies joining forces to bid for an overseas raw material asset. Indian companies are afraid to venture solo, worried as they are about the safety of their investment because of the Taliban threat. A consortium of Indian companies also went on to bid for mining copper and gold in Afghanistan in 2012 with the help of US technical expertise but was not successful.

India also piloted the move to make Afghanistan a member of the South Asian Association of Regional Cooperation (SAARC) with the hope that the entry of Afghanistan would help address issues relating to the transit and free flow of goods across borders in the region, thereby leading to greater economic development of Afghanistan and the region as a whole. India and Afghanistan both have an interest in the dismantling of trade and transit barriers to allow free movement of goods, investments and peoples across the region to engender constructive regional partnerships. Moreover, South Asia will be able to reach out to Central and West Asia more meaningfully with Afghanistan as a member of the SAARC. It has been estimated that given Afghanistan's low trade linkages with other states in the region, its participation in the South Asian Free Trade Area (SAFTA) would result in trade gains of $2 billion to the region, with as much as $606 million accruing to Afghanistan.[18] India's assistance programme as well as its support for an architecture of regional cooperation itself is aimed at helping Afghanistan emerge as a self-reliant nation, playing the role of a bridge linking the SAARC region with the larger Central Asia and making Afghanistan's neighbours stakeholders in its future. To help in generating industrial activity in Afghanistan, India not only worked towards restoring the industrial park in Pul-e-Charkhi but has also offered an EXIM Bank credit facility to small and medium Afghan enterprises.

Afghanistan has suggested that India become part of its trade and transit agreement with Pakistan, in force since 2011. This would allow India to use Pakistan's territory to trade with Afghanistan, enhancing regional connectivity and allowing sharing of economic dividends.[19] India hosted a conference of regional investors to mobilize support for Afghanistan's reconstruction and development in June 2012. It saw the participation of more than sixty-five private companies from over two dozen countries, including Pakistan, China, Russia, Iran and the US. This was the first conclave of its kind as it focused on promoting private sector investment from the region to rejuvenate and strengthen the Afghan economy. Exhorting the international community to invest in Afghanistan so as not to allow extremists to fill the vacuum after the withdrawal of Western forces in 2014,

New Delhi's message was: 'Let the grey suits of company executives take the place of olive green or desert brown fatigues of soldiers, and CEOs the place of generals.'[20] Underlying India's aid programme in Afghanistan, focusing largely on infrastructure and capacity-building projects, is a vision of 'an Afghanistan that will develop and leverage its resources for a better future; which will play the role of a transport and trading hub linking Central Asia with South Asia and beyond; and through which will flow trade, investment, energy and people, bringing benefits not just to the people of Afghanistan but also to the wider region'.[21]

Ordinary Afghans appear to have welcomed Indian involvement in development projects in their country. Almost 74 per cent of Afghans hold a favourable view of India compared to only 8 per cent who have a positive impression of Pakistan.[22] It has been India's deliberate policy to refrain from giving its support a military dimension and to stick to civilian matters. Western observers, though, tended to view Indian involvement in Afghanistan as problematic as it has worked to undercut Pakistan's influence in the country. The result was that, over time, India's attempt to leverage its 'soft power' in Afghanistan became increasingly risky.

PHASE II: NEW DELHI MARGINALIZED

As India's profile grew in Afghanistan, its adversaries, intent on ridding Afghanistan of Indian involvement, also upped the ante in an attempt to rupture burgeoning India–Afghanistan relations. This happened as the West got distracted by its war in Iraq, allowing the Taliban, with support from

Pakistan, to bounce back and reclaim the strategic space from which they had been ousted. As the balance of power shifted in favour of Pakistan and its proxies, Indian interests, including personnel and projects, emerged as viable targets. In July 2008, the Indian embassy in Kabul was struck by a blast that left sixty dead, including an Indian Foreign Service officer and an embassy defence attaché. In October 2009, a suicide car bombing outside the Indian embassy left at least seventeen dead and scores of others wounded.[23] Investigators soon concluded that the attack was perpetrated by the Pakistan-based Haqqani Network and suggested that Pakistani intelligence had also played a role. The Afghan envoy to the US underscored the involvement of Pakistani intelligence—the first time that a top Afghan official had openly blamed the ISI for a terrorist attack in his country.[24] India faced a tough road ahead as a perception gained ground that the Taliban were on the rebound with a heightened sense of political uncertainty in Washington about the future of American military presence in Afghanistan.

The return of the Taliban to Afghanistan would pose a major threat to its borders. In the end, the brunt of escalating terrorism would be borne by India as 'the sponge that protects' the West. Indian strategists have, for some time, been warning that a hurried US withdrawal, with the Taliban still posing a threat to Afghanistan, would have serious implications for India, not the least of which would be to see Pakistan, its eternal rival, step in more aggressively. To be fair, India's role in Afghanistan should not have been viewed through the eyes of Western observers, who dubbed India's Afghan engagement provocative for fear of offending

Pakistan, or through the eyes of Pakistan, which resented its own waning influence. Rather, India's involvement should have been considered through the eyes of the Afghan people, who had arguably benefited from the use of their neighbour's 'soft power', whatever its end motivations.

There has been a general consensus in India that it should not send troops to Afghanistan. Yet, beyond this, there was little agreement about what policy options it had if greater turbulence in the Af–Pak region spilled over into India. The traditional Indian stance had been that while India was happy to help the Afghan government in its reconstruction efforts, it would not be directly engaged in security operations, but this increasingly became harder to sustain. The inability of the Indian government to provide for the security of its private sector operating in Afghanistan led to a paradoxical situation, in which the Indian government's largest contractors in Afghanistan seemed to have participated in projects that might have ended up paying off the Haqqani Network, one of Afghanistan's deadliest and most anti-India insurgent groups.[25] A debate therefore started taking place as to whether India should start supporting its humanitarian endeavours in Afghanistan with a stronger military presence. If Afghanistan was the most important frontier in combating terrorism targeted at India, the critics asked, how long could India continue with its present policy trajectory whereby its civilians were killed in pursuit of its developmental objectives? This also started to have an impact on US–India relations. For too long, the Indian government seemed to have largely left the management of its neighbours to the US. A case in point was India's decision not to take any serious action against Pakistan in the aftermath of the 2008 Mumbai terrorist attacks, which killed 166 people and shattered India's self-confidence as a rising power. Instead, New Delhi continued to put pressure on Islamabad using American leverage to bring the masterminds of those terror strikes to justice and stop the use of Pakistani territory for terrorist violence directed at India, even though it was felt in New Delhi that this strategy was not really effective.

It was the sixty-nation London Conference on Afghanistan in January 2010 that advocated talks with the Taliban that jolted India, as New Delhi viewed with alarm its rapidly shrinking strategic space for diplomatic manoeuvring. When then Indian External Affairs Minister S.M. Krishna underscored the folly of making a distinction 'between a good Taliban and a bad Taliban' at the London Conference, he was completely out of sync with the larger mood at the conference.[26] The US-led Western alliance had made up its mind that it was not a question of if but when and how to exit from Afghanistan, which, to the leaders in Washington and London, was rapidly becoming a quagmire. So when it was decided in London that the time had come to woo the 'moderate' section of the Taliban back to share power in Kabul, it was a signal to India that Pakistan had convinced the West that it could play the role of mediator in negotiations with the Taliban, thereby underlining its centrality in the unfolding strategic dynamics in the region. It would be catastrophic for Indian security if remnants of the Taliban were to come to power with the backing of the ISI and Pakistan's military.

These changing ground realities forced India to start

reconsidering the terms of its involvement in Afghanistan. Pakistan's paranoia about Indian presence in Afghanistan had led the West to underplay India's largely beneficial role in the country, even as Pakistan's every claim about Indian intentions was being taken at face value. The Taliban militants who blew up the Indian embassy in Kabul in 2008 and tried again in 2009 had sent a strong signal that India was part of the evolving security dynamics in Afghanistan despite its reluctance to take on a more active role in military operations. After targeting personnel involved in developmental projects, and emboldened by India's non-response, these terrorists trained their guns directly at the Indian state by attacking its embassy. Moreover, as India's isolation at the London Conference underlined, its role in Afghanistan was not fully appreciated even by the West.

At the same time, Islamabad and Kabul also managed to formalize a pact in 2011, supported by the US, that would allow the Pakistani army a role in negotiating a reconciliation between Kabul and the Taliban.[27] The US publicly endorsed the idea of negotiations with the Taliban on a political settlement, with Washington holding several preliminary meetings with representatives of Mullah Omar, though without much progress. And as Pakistan succeeded in convincing the West that the best way out of the mess was to reach out to the 'good Taliban', India's marginalization seemed only to increase. Though the US and Afghan governments insisted that any settlement process should result in an end to Taliban violence and a willingness to conform to the Afghan constitution, the possibility of a Pakistan-sponsored settlement between hard-line elements

of the Taliban and the Afghan government became a serious
concern for India.

As the diplomatic cables released by WikiLeaks—a
whistleblower organization—in July 2010 underscored, India
was concerned about US plans to exit from Afghanistan and
its possible repercussions on India's security. Manmohan
Singh expressed his hope to the Obama administration
in 2009 that all those engaged in the process of moving
towards stability in Afghanistan would 'stay on course'.[28]
But the hope shattered as the US actively discouraged India
from assuming a higher profile in Afghanistan for fear of
offending Pakistan.[29] At the same time, it failed in getting
Pakistan to take Indian concerns more seriously. This led
to rapid deterioration of India's security environment, with
New Delhi having little or no strategic space to manoeuvre.
Not surprisingly, therefore, India was forced to reassess its
priorities vis-à-vis Af–Pak, given the huge stakes that New
Delhi had developed in Afghanistan over the previous decade.

Indian influence in Afghanistan had risen significantly
as American support for Pakistan shifted and Washington
demanded that Pakistan adopt policies that India had long
wanted in the immediate aftermath of 9/11. Moreover, India
had emerged as a major economic actor in Afghanistan
trying to bolster the Afghan state's capacity in various
measures. But by refusing to meld elements of hard and
soft power and to assert its profile more forcefully, India
soon made itself irrelevant as the ground realities changed
and a divergence emerged between the strategic interests
of India and Washington. A US intent on moving out of
Afghanistan managed to signal to Indian adversaries that

they could shape the post-American ground realities to serve their own ends. India lost the confidence of its own allies in Afghanistan. India's 'soft power' in Afghanistan had only resulted in soft targets for Pakistan-based terror groups. If India was unwilling to stand up for its own interests, few saw the benefit of aligning with India. The Indian presence only seemed to get weak with the Obama administration deepening its security dependence on Pakistan in the hope of achieving some semblance of success in Afghanistan.

Yet many in India continued to believe that the US would retain a substantive presence in Afghanistan so long as the mess in the Af–Pak area was not sorted out. But this was a dramatic misreading of Obama. He meant it when he said that America was not in the business of nation building over the next twenty years.

The Limits of Soft Power

Despite having a range of interests in Afghanistan, it has been clear that India's 'soft power' strategy of relying on political and economic engagement and cultural outreach, while making India one of the most popular foreign presences among ordinary Afghans, has not brought it any perceptible strategic gains. Rather, India stood sidelined by the West despite being the only country that has been relatively successful in winning the 'hearts and minds' of the Afghans. From the very beginning, the prime objective of India's Afghanistan policy was pre-empting the return of Pakistan's embedment in Afghanistan's strategic and political firmament. And ironically, it was India's success in

Afghanistan that drove Pakistan's security establishment into a panic mode, with a perception gaining ground that India was 'taking over Afghanistan'. The Obama administration's desire for a rapid withdrawal of American forces from Afghanistan gave the necessary opening to Pakistan to regain its lost influence in Kabul.[30] In order to keep Islamabad in good humour, Washington insisted on India limiting its role in Afghanistan. Washington seemed to have bought into Islamabad's argument that a large Indian presence in Afghanistan threatened Pakistan and made it difficult for it to cooperate fully with the international community in the fight against Al Qaeda and the Taliban. Yet India had a very limited presence in Afghanistan in the 1990s, and it was then that Pakistan had got a free hand in nurturing the Taliban.

India had much to consider. The return of the Taliban to Afghanistan would pose a major threat to its borders, and the brunt of escalating terrorism would be borne by India. As Henry Kissinger has put it, 'In many respects, India will be the most affected country if jihadist Islamism gains impetus in Afghanistan.'[31]

Karzai, meanwhile, grudgingly accepted a larger role for Pakistan in his country. His decision to send a contingent of Afghan military officers to Pakistan in July 2010 for training underlined his desire to seek a rapprochement with Islamabad.[32] The July 2011 deadline for the start of the withdrawal of US troops articulated by the Obama administration was intended to force Karzai to address urgent problems like corruption and ineffective governance. But it ended up having the opposite effect, convincing Karzai that soon he would be on his own. Though the US was at pains to underline that July 2011 'will be the beginning of a conditions-based process' of withdrawal of forces and that the deadline would be debated in the military's formal review of progress in December, there were few who were willing to bet that the Obama administration had the stomach to stay much longer in Afghanistan. Karzai, in particular, seemed convinced that Americans would not be able to stay the course.

Not surprisingly, Karzai started to craft a more autonomous foreign policy. He lost no time in dismissing two high-profile ministers—Interior Minister Abdul Rahim Wardak and intelligence chief Rahmatullah Nabeel—who were most closely allied with the US. These were the men Washington had insisted Karzai include in his cabinet after his re-election in 2009, and they had resisted his attempts to negotiate with the Taliban and forge closer ties with Islamabad. He now viewed Pakistan as an important player in ending the war through negotiations with the Taliban or on the battlefield. The decision to send officers for training in Pakistan was of great symbolic value and was the result of talks between the Afghan government and Pakistan's security agencies that began in May 2009. It was also reported that Karzai had a face-to-face meeting with Sirajuddin Haqqani, leader of the Haqqani Network, in the presence of Pakistan's army chief and the ISI chief.[33]

Taliban's growing power was evident in their dismissal of proposed negotiations with the US. They seemed convinced that they stood to win the war in Afghanistan and that public opinion in the West had turned against the war. As the central government in Kabul failed to expand its influence across the country, the Taliban used this political vacuum and growing disillusionment with the pace of development to reassert their authority by targeting foreign aid groups and attacking Western forces with greater ferocity.

Pakistan's security establishment relished its double game in Afghanistan. Pakistani support for the Taliban in Afghanistan continued to be sanctioned at the highest levels of Pakistan's government, with the ISI even represented on the Quetta Shura—the Taliban's war council—so as to retain influence over the Taliban's leadership. Taliban fighters continued to be trained in Pakistani camps. The ISI did not only provide financial, military and logistical support to the insurgency but it also retained strong strategic and operational control over the Taliban campaign in Afghanistan.[34] Despite launching offensives against militants in North and South Waziristan, Pakistani military continued to look upon the Taliban as a strategic asset. It continued to argue that its main priority was the Tehreek-e-Taliban (TTP) Pakistan—the Pakistani Taliban—and refused to do anything serious about the safe havens being used by the Al Qaeda, the Haqqani Network or the LeT.

In one of the largest single disclosures of such information in US history, WikiLeaks released more than 91,000 classified documents in July 2010, largely consisting of low-level field reports.[35] These documents also confirmed the long-held belief that Pakistan's intelligence agency continued to guide the Afghan insurgency even as it received more than $1 billion a year from Washington to combat the extremists. The ISI helped Afghan insurgents plan and carry out attacks on US forces in Afghanistan and their Afghan government allies. The efforts by the ISI to run the networks of suicide bombers and its help in organizing Taliban offensives at crucial periods in the Afghan war were also underlined.[36]

These revelations merely underscored what was widely known—that India had been systematically targeted by the ISI. The bombings of the Indian embassy in 2008 and 2009 had been at the behest of the ISI. It had paid the Haqqani Network to eliminate Indians working in Afghanistan as well as given orders to orchestrate attacks on Indian consulates in Afghanistan.[37] That the Pakistani security complex had engendered targeting of Indian interests in Afghanistan was hardly news in New Delhi. But what troubled Indian policymakers was Washington's reluctance to counter Pakistan's designs in Afghanistan.

Though India continued to insist that it would not retreat from Afghanistan, there were signs that it had started to scale down its presence. India's much-touted development partnership with Afghanistan started floundering because of India's inability to deliver on the ground, with significant delays in the completion of its development projects and investments. In the name of prudence, New Delhi decided to reduce the Indian presence and undertake only those projects that did not involve major deployment of manpower in Afghanistan.[38] Almost half of the Indian personnel working on various projects in Afghanistan returned by 2010. India did not take on any new projects, and various Indian schemes were put on hold. Training programmes for Afghan personnel started taking place in India. The conclusion of the Afghanistan–Pakistan Trade and Transit Agreement (APTTA), meanwhile, was a major shot in the arm for Pakistan as it explicitly affirmed that India would not be allowed to export goods to Afghanistan via the Wagah border.[39] Both Pakistan and Afghanistan had started hedging their bets against the coming US withdrawal.

At such a crucial juncture in its Afghanistan policy, New Delhi was not left with very many options as all the goodwill for India and support for its projects had not translated into any tangible gains for New Delhi in Afghanistan. India began debating its options in Afghanistan in a strategic space that had shrunken over the years. By failing to craft its own narrative on Af–Pak ever since US troops went into Afghanistan in the aftermath of 11 September 2001, New Delhi had allowed the West, and increasingly Pakistan, to dictate the contours of Indian policy towards the region. It was time for India to change tack. But the options were few, and there was a low likelihood that they would succeed in giving New Delhi a credible presence in Afghanistan post-2014.

CHAPTER 4

BACK IN THE GAME: TOO LITTLE, TOO LATE?

'I think it is too early for the Americans to give us the full picture. Afghans themselves are unable to give the full picture. I have been to the Heart of Asia conference, and, apart from the fact that everybody was clearly remaining committed to the future of Afghanistan, as we do, there are no clear roadmaps about what can happen during 2014.'

—Salman Khurshid, former Indian external affairs minister, in July 2013

PHASE III: INDIA FIGHTS BACK

TO PRESERVE ITS INTERESTS AND retain some credibility in a rapidly evolving strategic milieu where New Delhi had been marginalized, India was forced to take a number of policy measures vis-à-vis Afghanistan. These included a decision to step up its role in the training of Afghan forces, achieving greater policy coordination with states like Russia and Iran, and reaching out to all sections of Afghan society.[1]

A Strategic Partnership with Kabul

As the strategic realities in South Asia radically altered in the aftermath of the killing of Osama bin Laden—Al Qaeda founder and the brain behind 9/11—then Indian Prime Minister Manmohan Singh lost no time in reaching out to Afghanistan with his two-day visit to Kabul after a six-year absence. He announced a fresh commitment of $500 million for Afghanistan's development, over and above India's existing aid assistance of around $1.5 billion.[2] New Delhi and Kabul agreed that the 'strategic partnership' between the two neighbours, to be implemented under the framework of a partnership council headed by the foreign ministers of the two nations, will entail cooperation in areas of security, law enforcement and justice, including an enhanced focus on cooperation in the fight against international terrorism, organized crime, illegal trafficking in narcotics, and money laundering.

Most significant of all was Singh's expression of India's support for the Afghan government's plan of national reconciliation involving Taliban insurgents, thereby signally an end to India's public opposition to a deal with the Taliban and bridging a strategic gap with the US.[3] Also, shedding its reticence on Afghan security issues, India became more outspoken about its commitment to build the capabilities of the Afghan security forces.[4] New Delhi's review of its regional foreign policy priorities couldn't have come at a more urgent time.

In a rare honour, Singh addressed a joint session of the Afghan parliament, underscoring Indo-Afghan unity in fighting extremism. Describing bin Laden's death as a 'unique moment', Singh tried to use India's political capital to reinforce New Delhi's centrality in the region's evolving strategic realities. Only weeks ago, the Pakistani military had urged Kabul to dump the US and look instead to Pakistan and its ally China for help in striking a peace deal with the Taliban and rebuilding the economy. And a month back, Kabul and Islamabad had announced the establishment of a two-tier joint commission that gave the Pakistani military a formal role in reconciliation talks between Kabul and Pakistan-based insurgents.

Singh's visit was followed by the signing of a landmark strategic partnership agreement between New Delhi and Kabul during Karzai's visit to New Delhi in October 2011. It committed India to 'training, equipping and capacity building' of the Afghan security forces. India pledged to train and equip Afghanistan's army and police force, expanding on the limited training it conducted for the army in India in 2007. India acceded to Afghanistan's request for 150 army officers to receive training at Indian defence and military academies and also agreed to begin hosting training sessions for Afghan police officers.[5] This was Afghanistan's first strategic pact with any country, though Karzai later signed such pacts with the US and the NATO to ward off the challenge from Pakistan. As part of the new pact, bilateral dialogue at the level of the national security advisor was institutionalized to focus on enhancing cooperation in security issues. New Delhi hoped that Kabul would take the lead in defining the exact terms of this engagement even as it made it clear that India would 'stand by Afghanistan' when foreign troops withdrew from the country in 2014.

Along with the strategic pact, two other agreements on Indo-Afghan cooperation in developing hydrocarbons and mineral resources were signed, further underlining India's role in the evolution of Afghanistan as a viable economic unit. The two nations agreed to enhance political cooperation and institutionalize regular bilateral political and foreign office consultations. Underscoring its role as Afghanistan's main economic partner, India in June 2012 hosted the Delhi Investment Summit on Afghanistan, where it called upon the private sector to invest in Afghanistan 'to create a virtuous cycle of healthy economic competition in Afghanistan'[6]. The strategic pact with India was Afghanistan's way of trying to deal with an increasingly more menacing Pakistan. During his visit to New Delhi, Karzai was categorical in suggesting that South Asia faced 'dangers from terrorism and extremism used as an instrument of policy against innocent civilians'.

Afghanistan's relationship with Pakistan deteriorated after Karzai decided to call off nascent peace talks with Taliban militants. After calling the Taliban 'brothers' and encouraging the insurgents to reconcile with the Afghan government, Karzai became more hard-nosed in his appraisal of the Taliban and its sponsors in Pakistan. He suggested that peace talks with the Taliban were futile unless they involved the Pakistani authorities who were the real masters behind the operations of the insurgent groups.[7] His attitude was particularly affected by the killing in September 2011 of former Afghan President Burhanuddin Rabbani, the Afghan government's chief peace envoy, by the Taliban. Kabul was categorical that this assassination was plotted in the Pakistani city of Quetta with the active support of the ISI.

Though many in Washington viewed bin Laden's killing as an opening that could be used to accelerate a negotiated settlement with the Taliban and hasten the end of the Afghan war, US–Pakistan ties too went into a nosedive soon thereafter. The security establishment in Pakistan wanted to retain Pakistan's central role in negotiations with the Taliban and prevent the US from having any long-term military presence in Afghanistan. Meanwhile, Washington signalled that it would not tolerate continuing use of terrorist groups, aided and abetted by the ISI, to kill Americans and their allies in Afghanistan. In a radical departure from the long-standing US policy of publicly playing down Pakistan's official support for insurgents operating from havens within Pakistan, Admiral Mike Mullen, then chairman of the US Joint Chiefs of Staff, described the Haqqani Network as a 'veritable arm' of Pakistan's ISI.[8] Pakistan's sponsorship of the Haqqani Network had been an open secret for quite some time as was the fact that the Haqqanis were responsible for some of the most murderous assaults on Indian and Western presence in Afghanistan. The US was reluctant to take on Pakistan on this issue until such time as American interests did not come under direct attack. And when they did, Washington had little choice but to confront Pakistan's civilian and military leaders.

As the West outlined its plans for a pullout from Afghanistan, New Delhi recognized the immediacy of strengthening its partnership with Kabul. Strengthening the security dimension of India–Afghanistan ties was extremely important for India as it was in New Delhi's interest to help Kabul preserve its strategic autonomy at a time when Pakistan had made it clear that it would like the Haqqani Network and the Taliban to be at the centre of the post-American political dispensation in Kabul. Moreover, India had emerged as a favourite target of the extremists in Afghanistan. As mentioned earlier, the Indian embassy in Kabul was attacked twice, in 2008 and 2009, killing around seventy-five people. In 2010, two Kabul guest houses popular among Indians were attacked, killing more than six Indians. In 2013, a botched bombing targeting the Indian consulate in Jalalabad killed nine people. And then in May 2014, the Indian consulate in western Afghanistan's Herat province came under assault. Most of these attacks were traced back to the Haqqani Network and the LeT.

At the same time, it is true that, given the logic of geography and demography, Pakistan cannot be ignored in the future viability of Afghanistan. India and Afghanistan can change the conditions on the ground by forcing Pakistan to acknowledge that its policy towards its neighbours has not only brought instability to the region but also pushed the very existence of Pakistan into question. Karzai assuaged Pakistani anxieties when he suggested in 2011 that 'Pakistan is a twin brother' while 'India is a great friend'. New Delhi launched a major effort towards the capability enhancement of the Afghan National Army (ANA) to help it handle the internal security of Afghanistan after the departure of Western forces. The number of ANA personnel being trained in Indian Army institutions jumped from 574 in 2012-13 to well over 1,000 in 2013-14.[9] Meanwhile, as Kabul and Washington decided to make moves towards negotiations with the Taliban, New Delhi also signalled that it was willing to engage with sections of the Taliban. The questions remained, however, if it was possible to differentiate between the so-called 'reconcilable' and irreconcilable elements of the insurgents in Afghanistan and if even the reconcilable ones were really interested in negotiations at a time when they seemed to be winning.

Forging New Alignments

Even as New Delhi reached out to Kabul for a strengthened security partnership, it also recognized the need to coordinate more closely with states such as Russia and Iran, with which it shared convergent interests vis-à-vis Afghanistan and Pakistan. None of these states would accept a fundamentalist Sunni-dominated regime in Kabul or the re-emergence of Afghanistan as a base for jihadist terrorism directed at neighbouring states. The Indian government reached out to Moscow at the highest political levels, reiterating the two nations' shared positions on Afghanistan and institutionalizing cooperation on this issue.[10] Where India recognized that a victory by pro-Pakistan Pashtun groups, Taliban or otherwise, in Afghanistan as a defeat of its outreach to Afghans, Russia hoped to leverage the Afghan crisis into an acceptance of Moscow's security leadership by the Central Asian nations vulnerable to Taliban-inspired Islamist militancy.

Moscow, for its part, having kept itself aloof from

Afghanistan and Pakistan for years after the Taliban's ouster, refocused on Afghanistan as Islamist extremism and drug trafficking emanating from Central Asia re-emerged as major threats to its national security. It hosted the presidents of Afghanistan, Pakistan and Tajikistan in August 2010, promised to invest heavily in developing Afghan infrastructure and natural resources, and repeatedly laid down certain 'red lines' for the Taliban's integration into the political process, notably renunciation of violence, cessation of the armed struggle, acceptance of the Afghan constitution, and a complete break with the Al Qaeda.[11]

During then Russian President Vladimir Putin's visit to India in December 2002, even as Russia secured India's agreement to intensify the strategic partnership, India was able to receive Russian support on its position on Pakistan, with Russia calling on Pakistan to end its support for cross-border terrorism.[12] The Russian endorsement of the Indian position on terrorism and Pakistan reflected the Russian desire to maintain the traditional goodwill in relations by politically genuflecting to India's deepest security concerns. Russia repeatedly called upon Pakistan to do more on terrorism directed at India, and, in 2010, the joint statement signed during then President Dmitry Medvedev's visit to Delhi named Pakistan categorically for the first time.[13]

The two states remained concerned about the deteriorating security situation in Afghanistan, where, they argued, successful stabilization would be possible only after the elimination of safe havens and infrastructure for terrorism and violent extremism present in Pakistan and Afghanistan. As Russia sought to find a role in the aftermath of the withdrawal of NATO forces, it also made it clear that, much like India, it too did not favour a quick withdrawal of foreign troops and even facilitated the transit of military supplies for NATO forces in Afghanistan through its territory.[14] Russia's deputy defence minister suggested in 2013 that the West 'has been too hasty about making the final decision to pull out'. Highlighting Russia's serious concerns on the evolving situation in Afghanistan after the departure of NATO troops in 2014, its Deputy Prime Minister Dmitry Rogozin suggested in 2012 that India and Russia would have to work together to manage regional security as 'thousands of terrorists and fundamentalists will seek refuge in Afghanistan as well as the region around the country' and this would 'change the situation drastically around the region and for countries like Tajikistan, Kazakhstan and Central Asia'[15].

During Manmohan Singh's visit to Russia in October 2013, the two sides emphasized that Pakistan's attempt to bring back the Taliban into Afghan political structures was an outcome not acceptable to the two states. India and Russia also began working together to revive an arms maintenance factory in Afghanistan in a sign of their stepped-up engagement in Afghan security.[16] Russia has been trying to increase its military and economic ties with Afghanistan even as it has been busy enhancing its military presence in various Central Asian states.

Russia and India's geopolitical and security interests in the Central Asian region are also compatible in so far as religious extremism, terrorism, drug trafficking, smuggling in small arms, and organized crime emanating largely from Central Asia threaten both countries equally. As a consequence, Russia has been pushing for a full membership of India in the Shanghai Cooperation Organization (SCO). The SCO was founded in Shanghai in 2001 by the presidents of Russia, China, Kyrgyz Republic, Kazakhstan, Tajikistan and Uzbekistan. India was admitted as an observer at the 2005 Astana Summit along with Iran and Pakistan. The group's members, including Russia, China, and most Central Asian states, share intelligence and conduct joint military exercises even if they fail to coordinate larger policy because of competing interests.

The SCO plans to focus more on Afghanistan and Pakistan in the coming years, given a rising anxiety among neighbouring states that extremist and terrorist forces will find a fresh opportunity to gain traction once the US and allied forces leave Afghanistan. In May 2013, Putin called on the SCO to assume a greater role in defending its member states from extremism emanating from Afghanistan. The SCO membership will allow India greater leverage in shaping the ground realities in Afghanistan. The SCO could provide the regional framework for the stabilization of Afghanistan as all of its neighbours except Turkmenistan are members of the SCO in one form or another. The US itself has started a dialogue process with the SCO.

Russia and India will have to work together to avert a destabilizing power vacuum in Afghanistan if a blowback of terrorism from the Af–Pak region is to be avoided.[17] India has repeatedly underscored its desire to seek 'full member' status in the SCO and made it clear that India remains keen on deepening security-related cooperation with it, particularly with the SCO's Regional Anti-Terrorism Structure (RATS).

Both New Delhi and Moscow agree that the key to resolving Afghanistan is a regional solution wherein all neighbours ensure that Afghanistan controls its own future and no one intervenes in its internal politics. India has maintained that the SCO should 'step up its engagement in the rebuilding and reconstruction of Afghanistan through common projects and financial commitments. India would then support the efforts by Russia to craft common SCO positions on Afghanistan'. Considering terrorism is a major threat to the security and stability of Afghanistan, New Delhi has been underlining that a long-term solution can be 'achieved by supporting the efforts made by Afghanistan itself to begin an Afghan-led dialogue on reconciliation with the armed opposition forces, provided that these groups respect the principles adopted by the international community'[18].

India has long wanted to play a larger role in the SCO and has been seeking support from individual member states for quite some time. However, New Delhi has not been successful in achieving an upgrade in its observer status. The organization has failed to achieve a consensus on India's role in the grouping. It is not very difficult to see why this should be the case. China remains reluctant to see India as a full member of the group despite its official rhetoric that it wants to see India play a larger role. Though the 2010 Tashkent Summit lifted the moratorium on new membership, India's role in the grouping remains a marginal one.

Iran is the other nation India has been reaching out to, with New Delhi's outreach to Tehran becoming more serious after signals from the Iranians that the relationship was drifting. The two countries had worked closely when the

Taliban was in power in Kabul and continued to cooperate on several infrastructure projects allowing transit facilities for Indian goods, but the Indian decision to vote against Iran at the International Atomic Energy Agency (IAEA) in 2005-06 on the Iranian nuclear issue led to a chilling of the bilateral relationship.[19] Although India believes that Iran has the right to pursue its civilian nuclear energy programme, it has insisted that Iran clarify the doubts raised by the IAEA regarding its compliance with the Non-Proliferation Treaty. India has long maintained that it does not see further nuclear proliferation as being in its interests. This position has as much to do with India's desire to project itself as a responsible nuclear state as with the very real danger that further proliferation in its extended neighbourhood could endanger its security. India has continued to affirm its commitment to enforce all sanctions against Iran as mandated since 2006 by the UN Security Council when the first set of sanctions was imposed.

However, much like Beijing and Moscow, New Delhi has argued that such sanctions should not hurt the Iranian populace and expressed its disapproval of sanctions by individual countries that restrict investments by third countries in Iran's energy sector. New Delhi has made an effort to revive its partnership with Tehran on Afghanistan, with the two sides deciding to hold 'structured and regular consultations' on the issue of Afghanistan.[20] For its part, Tehran was worried about the potential major role for leaders of the almost exclusively Sunni Taliban in the emerging political order in Afghanistan. It even encouraged New Delhi to send more assistance to provinces in northern and western Afghanistan that are under the control of those associated with the Northern Alliance. At the Iranians' initiative, India became part of a trilateral Afghan–Iranian–Indian effort in 2010 to counter Pakistan's attempts to freeze India out of various regional initiatives.[21] In defiance of the international sanctions, the Indian government even started encouraging Indian companies to invest in the Iranian energy sector so that economic interests could underpin the bilateral political realignment.[22]

India and Iran signed an agreement to set up a joint working group on terrorism and security, the main purpose of which was to share intelligence on Al Qaeda activities in Afghanistan. Both countries have a shared interest in a stable Afghanistan with a regime that is not only fully representative of the ethnic and cultural diversity of Afghanistan but also capable of taking the country on the path of economic development and social stability, thereby enhancing the security of the entire region. Defence ties between India and Iran also evolved after the signing of a memorandum of understanding on defence cooperation by the two in 2001. Though this cooperation was mostly restricted to training and exchange of visits, India also used Iranian ports to send aid to Afghanistan, given Pakistan's denial of access to India. Even as the US conducted its war games in the Persian Gulf in March 2007, its largest show of force in the region since the 2003 invasion of Iraq involving the USS *Eisenhower* and USS *Stennis*, the Iranian naval chief visited India, a reflection of the importance that Iran attached to its growing defence ties with India. This visit reportedly resulted in the establishment of a joint defence working group to look into Tehran's request that India train its military personnel.

Iran remains India's only corridor to the Central Asian republics, given India's adversarial relations with Pakistan. In return for Iran's provision to India of the transit facilities, India helped Iran improve its transportation facilities like ports and railways. India cooperated with Iran in the development of a new port complex at Chabahar on the coast of Iran, which could become India's gateway to Afghanistan and Central Asia. Another project involved linking the Chabahar port to the Iranian rail network that is well connected to Central Asia and Europe. What was significant about these projects was that Pakistan would become marginal to India's relationship with the Central Asian region. The emergence of the Gwadar port, which Pakistan is developing with China's help, has been overshadowed by the strategically significant Chabahar. The contest is on between Iran and Pakistan to become the favoured commercial and energy intermediary for the Central Asian republics. This contest between the two ports could well reduce Pakistan's logistical leverage on Afghanistan with the completion of the Zaranj–Delaram road.

Moreover, India's plan to build a highway linking the southern Afghan city of Kandahar to Zahidan was of concern to Pakistan as it would reduce Afghanistan's dependence on Pakistan to the benefit of Iran. India's building of roads in Afghanistan was seen as particularly worrisome as it would increase the influence of India and Iran and boost Afghanistan's connectivity to the outside world. India also hoped that the road link through Afghanistan and Iran would open up markets for its goods in Afghanistan and beyond in Central Asia.

India wanted to increase its presence in the Iranian energy

sector because of its rapidly rising energy needs and was rightfully restless about its own marginalization in Iran. Not only did Pakistan sign a pipeline deal with Tehran in 2010 but China also started to make its presence felt there. Surpassing the European Union, China became Iran's largest trading partner in 2010 and undertook massive investments in the country, rapidly occupying the space vacated by Western firms. While Beijing's economic engagement with Iran grew, India's presence shrank as firms such as Reliance Industries withdrew from Iran, partially under Western pressure, and others shelved their plans to make investments. Indian oil companies found it hard to get vessels to lift Iranian cargo because of Western sanctions. The Shipping Corporation of India, India's largest domestic tanker owner, refused to provide its tankers to Indian Oil Corporation for lifting Iranian oil. Consequently, Iran's share in Indian oil imports has been declining, with Iraq replacing Iran as the second largest crude oil supplier to India in 2013.

At the same time, there was little evidence that Iran would be a reliable partner in India's search for energy security. Iran either rejected or did not finalize plans due to last-minute changes in the terms and conditions for a number of important projects with Indian businesses and the Indian government. Moreover, two major energy deals signed with great fanfare raised concerns in the West and failed to take off. The first was India's twenty-five-year, $22 billion agreement with Iran for the export of liquefied natural gas (LNG). It did not lead to anything since it was signed in 2005 as it required India to build an LNG plant in Iran with American components, which would have violated the US's

Iran and Libya Sanctions Act. The other project involved the construction of a 2,775-km, $7 billion pipeline to carry natural gas from Iran to India via Pakistan.

After India reduced its oil imports from Iran from 18 million tonnes in 2011-12 to 13.3 million tonnes in 2012-13 as Western sanctions made payments in foreign currency impossible, Iran tried to woo India back by offering oilfields on lucrative terms, routing the gas pipeline through the sea to avoid Pakistan and insurance to refiners. Alternatively, Iran offered to ship the gas in its liquid form (LNG) via Oman.[23]

India's foreign policy towards Iran is multifaceted and a function of a number of variables, including India's energy requirements, its outreach to the Muslim world, its large Shia population and its policy on Afghanistan. There has been a lot of hyperbole about India–Iran ties, which some Western analysts have described as an 'axis', a 'strategic partnership', or even an 'alliance'. The Indian Left made Iran an issue emblematic of India's 'strategic autonomy' and used the bogey of toeing an American line on Iran to coerce New Delhi into following an ideological and anti-American foreign policy. A close examination of the India–Iran relationship, however, reveals an underdeveloped relationship despite all the spin attached to it. Where India's stakes are growing rapidly in the Persian Gulf, India's ties with Iran remain circumscribed by the internal power struggle and economic decay in Iran, growing tensions between Iran and its Arab neighbours, and Iran's continued defiance of the global nuclear order.[24] But the future of Afghanistan took centre stage in Indo-Iranian ties as the security situation started deteriorating and plans for Western withdrawal firmed up.

It is not often appreciated how important the Af–Pak issue is to India's future security, its strategic planning, and its relationship with Iran. The uncertainty surrounding the future of Afghanistan forced India to keep its ties with Iran on an even keel and coordinate more closely with Iran as a contingency plan. If the US does decide to leave Afghanistan with Pakistan retaining its pre-2001 leverage, New Delhi and Tehran will likely be drawn closer together to counteract Islamabad's influence in Kabul that had been largely detrimental to their interests in the past. In this context, the rapprochement between the US and Iran after the coming to office in 2013 of a moderate Hassan Rouhani as Iran's president, succeeding the hard-liner Mahmoud Ahmadinejad, opened up diplomatic space for India.

Just after Iran sealed an initial accord in November 2013 with six powers, including the US, to limit its nuclear programme in exchange for the easing of some sanctions, Indian Foreign Secretary Sujatha Singh met Iranian Deputy Foreign Minister Ebrahim Rahimpour to discuss economic opportunities. Plans were in place to speed up the work on the Chabahar port in south-eastern Iran which could be connected to the Zaranj–Delaram road in Afghanistan's Nimroz province via Milak, also built with Indian assistance. Despite American pressure, India decided to pump in $100 million for the upgrade of Chabahar in May 2013, not only to get easier access for Indian goods into Central Asia but also to counter the China–Pakistan axis in the Indian Ocean after Islamabad decided to hand over the operational control of its Gwadar port to China.[25] This would also help in circumventing the problems of Pakistan's continuing denial of access to Indian shipments bound for Afghanistan as well as lower Afghanistan's dependence on Pakistani ports.

New Delhi also sought reassurances from Moscow and Tehran that the three states were in unanimity on Afghanistan and Pakistan. It remained to be seen, however, if India's gravitation towards Russia and Iran would be enough to arrest the slide of the situation in Af–Pak to India's detriment.

Managing Pakistan

Finally, India also realized there was no alternative to direct talks with Pakistan if a regional solution to the Afghanistan conundrum was to be found. New Delhi restarted talks with Pakistan in 2010 after suspending them in the aftermath of the terrorist attacks in Mumbai in November 2008, and these included back-channel negotiations with the Pakistani military. While these attempts failed to produce anything concrete, the hope in New Delhi was that they would at least stave off pressure from the US to engage Islamabad. Therefore, even though negotiations with Pakistan were hugely unpopular at home, the Indian government decided to proceed with them. India hoped that by doing so, it would be viewed as a more productive player in the West's efforts at stabilizing Afghanistan.

There remain several impediments to long-term India–Pakistan peace, but the Pakistani civilian leadership signalled its desire for a rapprochement with India. The Asif Ali Zardari government made some positive moves, which New Delhi showed a willingness to reciprocate. Most significant of Pakistani initiatives was a decision in 2012 to finally grant the

Most Favoured Nation (MFN) status to India after years of failing to reciprocate India's decision to do the same in 1996.[26] This was not a radical decision as the terms and conditions of the World Trade Organization require member states to bestow the MFN status on each other so that there is no discrimination and all states benefit equally from the lowest possible tariffs. And yet the move by Pakistan was politically significant as the Pakistani government signalled that it was indeed serious about the dialogue process with India.

Both New Delhi and Islamabad realized that a lack of dialogue between the two neighbours had become counterproductive. Since 1996, Pakistan had linked the MFN issue with the contentious issue of Kashmir, and, in the absence of the MFN status to India, around 20,000 Indian export items to Pakistan had to be routed through a third nation. With the granting of the MFN status, it was estimated that bilateral trade could jump to $8 billion from the paltry $3 billion over five years.[27] This made the move an important confidence-building measure that would allow the two sides to take their dialogue forward on other more contentious issues. Islamabad announced its decision suggesting that 'all stakeholders, including our [Pakistan's] military and defence institutions, were on board'. India, not surprisingly, welcomed the decision, arguing that 'economic engagements, trade, removing barriers to trade and facilitating land transportation would help the region'.

For some time, there had been growing support in Pakistan for normalizing trade ties with India. When Asif Ali Zardari became the president in 2008, he had articulated the need for greater economic cooperation with India but was rebuffed by the all-powerful military. Pakistan soon came under tremendous pressure to prove its credentials as a responsible regional player in light of the crisis in Afghanistan and rapidly deteriorating internal security situation. Pakistan's economy was in a parlous condition, with growth down to 3.7 per cent in 2012, the lowest growth rate in South Asia. External sources of funding also became difficult to come by. After Islamabad declined to pursue the advice of the International Monetary Fund (IMF) to expand its tax base in March 2010, the fund decided to suspend disbursement of its $11 billion facility.

Its ties with the US too deteriorated sharply after May 2011 when the US Navy Seals killed bin Laden in Abbottabad, Pakistan. The Obama administration's decision to suspend a portion of the US aid to the Pakistani military led many in Islamabad to become even more forceful in underlining Beijing's importance for Pakistan. Reacting to the US move of cutting aid, Islamabad's then ambassador to Beijing, Masood Khan, was quick to suggest that 'China will stand by us in difficult times as it has been doing for the past years'[28]. But Chinese involvement in Pakistan was unlikely to match the US profile in the country in the short to medium term, and it was not readily evident if China even wanted to match the US in this regard.[29]

This led Pakistan to explore new foreign policy options, and a more pragmatic approach towards India was one of the outcomes. Normalizing trade relations with India allowed Pakistan to not only garner economic benefits from one of the world's fastest growing economies but also to alter the impression of being the perpetual troublemaker. This was followed by a pact on a new visa regime between India and Pakistan that would ease travel restrictions for businessmen and introduce a new category of group tourism as well as provisions of visa on arrival for persons aged above sixty-five.[30] These moves are unlikely to resolve the fundamental conflict between the two rivals, but it was a start that the two sides hoped to build on. Yet, for all the hype that the apparent move by Pakistan to grant India MFN status generated, it turned out to be a damp squib when first Pakistan made it clear that India was unlikely to be granted the MFN status before the 2014 Lok Sabha elections and resumption of composite dialogue between the two nations and then indefinitely postponed the decision on account of resistance from the military and domestic trade groups.

The larger peace process between India and Pakistan, however, primarily hinged on the ability of Pakistan's political establishment to prevent terrorist groups from wreaking havoc on India. There was little evidence of any significant Pakistani effort to dismantle the infrastructure of terrorism such as communications, launching pads and training camps on its eastern border with India. Even if it wanted to, the civilian government in Islamabad would not be able to exert much control, given that various terrorist outfits would continue their jihad in Kashmir. Moreover, Pakistan gave India no credible reassurance about either bringing the masterminds of the Mumbai attacks to justice or refraining from using terrorism as an instrument of state policy against India.

Meanwhile, in India, the then Congress-led government in New Delhi found it difficult to make any significant concessions on Kashmir as it faced pressure from the right of the political establishment. This was especially difficult after the Mumbai attacks as no party wanted to be viewed as responsible for going soft on Pakistan if there was another attack—a perception that could spring from concluding a deal with Pakistan before another incident. As a result, while there was general consensus on smaller steps like opening bus routes or trade with Pakistan, this did not translate into willingness to sign a broader settlement. The Indian government accused Pakistan of helping terrorists to infiltrate Indian territory while the Pakistani government ratcheted up pressure on India by raising the issue of Kashmir at the United Nations, thereby underlining its centrality to India–Pakistan ties.[31]

And the virulence of anti-India groups in Pakistan continued unabated. After India hanged Ajmal Kasab in 2012, the sole terrorist who was captured alive at the scene of violence on 26 November 2008 in Mumbai, the TTP threatened to avenge his death by striking Indian targets anywhere and the Jamat-ud-Da'wah (JuD), which India holds responsible for carrying out the Mumbai terror attacks, reportedly offered funeral prayers in absentia for Kasab.[32] The LeT, the Pakistani militant group accused of masterminding the Mumbai attacks, meanwhile, suggested that Kasab was a 'hero' whose death will 'inspire other fighters to follow his path'[33]. The LeT was also later accused of being behind the May 2014 attack on the Indian consulate in Herat by the Afghan government.

For many in the policy establishment in New Delhi, Islamabad does not seem ready for peace, and the Pakistani military and intelligence establishment is not at all favourably inclined to accept any role for India in Afghanistan.[34] India–Pakistan engagement on Afghanistan remains perfunctory at best. The Pakistani military hopes to dominate Afghanistan through its proxies, but there are groups that have even targeted the Pakistani military. The gap between Pakistan's strategic aspiration to control the internal politics of Afghanistan and its patent inability to pacify some of the groups like the TTP has grown in recent years.

The Nawaz Sharif government, despite the occasional rhetoric, is yet to give a serious indication that it is willing to take a risk in nurturing positive ties with India or that it is willing to take on the 'spoilers'—those elements in the Pakistani military and its non-state proxies who remain intent on derailing the Indo-Pak dialogue process. In fact, the day Sharif visited New Delhi for the swearing-in of the Narendra Modi government on 26 May 2014, Pakistani rangers fired at Indian troops on the border, and, days before, the Indian consulate in Herat had come under attack from LeT operatives in Afghanistan, all intended to create a crisis ahead of the taking over by the new Indian government and to unequivocally underscore that Pakistan's India policy remained firmly under the Pakistani army's control.

As the Modi government took charge, it was expected to continue with the policy of limited outreach to Islamabad. But it was not evident if Indian attempts at redefining the terms of its engagement in Pakistan at the very late stage would produce an outcome conducive to protecting and enhancing Indian interests in Afghanistan. This was especially true in a context in which the extant regional environment precluded any possibility of a sustainable outcome for Afghanistan.

CHAPTER 5

REGIONAL REALITIES: AS COMPLICATED AS EVER

'We need a just and enduring peace, not a quick deal with the Taliban. The Taliban talk about girls' education and political pluralism now, but they think that after the NATO troops withdraw, they can conquer and rule us again … We will never sacrifice a single Afghan's rights just to get settlement with the Taliban.'

—Ismael Qasimyar, Afghan Peace Council member, in May 2013

ALL MAJOR REGIONAL PLAYERS AND global powers are struggling to come to terms with the aftermath of the withdrawal of NATO-led Western military forces from Afghanistan. Regional cooperation, time and again, has been declared as the only viable alternative to the festering regional tensions that have plagued the country for decades. Various South and Central Asian governments, for example, have underscored that they recognize that Afghanistan's problems of terrorism, narcotics trafficking and corruption affect them all and have to be addressed through cooperative efforts. In November 2011, they adopted the Istanbul Protocol that committed countries as diverse as China, India, Iran, Kazakhstan, Pakistan and Russia to cooperation in countering terrorism, drug trafficking and insurgency in Afghanistan and in the neighbouring areas.[1] In this context, Afghanistan's traditionally divisive neighbours pledged to support its efforts to reconcile with insurgent groups and to work together on joint security and economic initiatives to build long-term Afghan stability. The participants embraced a new Silk Road strategy that envisages a dynamic Afghanistan at the heart of South and Central Asian trade and economic relationships.

The Istanbul effort was touted as a regional endeavour to solve a major regional issue, and the very fact that so many regional states came together to at least articulate a policy response was indeed a step in the right direction. The US also reached out to regional powers in order to bring them into Afghanistan more substantively. Former Special US Representative for Afghanistan and Pakistan James F. Dobbins and his successor Daniel Feldman engaged governments in the region to assess the role they could play in bringing long-term peace to the country. The Afghan government too underlined the role of regional cooperation in securing peace in the country. Afghanistan's ambassador to India, Shaida Abdali, made clear in 2012: 'In the months and years ahead, the opportunity to further secure and develop Afghanistan will widen for regional leadership and cooperation. We look forward to working with India and our other neighbours to consolidate the collective gains made towards durable peace in Afghanistan. Collective success is very much within our reach in Afghanistan. But it will only result from sincere cooperation among all our neighbours.'[2]

But the practical difficulties in implementing the vision of regional cooperation remained as stark as ever because of regional power struggles. Turkey, for example, made a public effort to try to mediate between Pakistan and Afghanistan. As a result of this, Karzai and Zardari agreed to a joint inquiry into the assassination of Burhanuddin Rabbani, who was in charge of negotiations with the Taliban as head of Afghanistan's High Peace Council. But it did not lead to a significant normalization of ties between Islamabad and Kabul. Meanwhile, Central Asian states remained worried that extremist groups based in Pakistan and Afghanistan were trying to infiltrate Central Asia in order to launch terrorist attacks.

Other regional players have their own interests in the future of Afghanistan. Iran opposes any long-term American presence in Afghanistan, while Russia wants to ensure that Afghanistan doesn't become the source of Islamist instability that can be transported to its territories via other Central Asian states. China wants to preserve its growing economic profile in Afghanistan but is not interested in making significant political investment at the moment. It hopes it can rely on its 'all-weather' friend in Pakistan to meet its interests in Af–Pak. India shares common interests with the regional states with respect to Afghanistan but is unlikely to find support from them given the nature of regional power realities. And this contributes to India's Afghan muddle. China shares common interests with India in Afghanistan but doesn't want to realize them at the cost of its friendship with Pakistan. India and Iran also have converging interests but a common vision vis-à-vis Afghanistan continues to elude them. Further, Iran seems ready to support any group, even the Taliban, which can fight US presence in Afghanistan. Russia could move closer to Pakistan in the wake of India–US rapprochement. And Pakistan itself will continue supporting anti-India Taliban and other extremist groups in Afghanistan. Regional cooperation on Afghanistan, as desirable as it is, cannot be a strategy that New Delhi can rely on to stabilize Afghanistan and secure its interests. It's a complete dead end as the regional power configuration makes it highly unlikely that Afghanistan's neighbours will have a unifying vision for the region any time soon.

CHINA'S AMBIGUOUS ROLE

Some in the Indian strategic community have suggested that China shares a range of objectives with India, including a prosperous, sustainable, and secure Pakistan that does not remain a base for Al Qaeda and its affiliates.[3] The rapidly deteriorating situation in Pakistan and its long-term consequences for regional stability might, some suggest, result in greater cooperation between Beijing and New Delhi to stabilize the shared periphery between the two nations. Turbulence in Xinjiang, such as the riots between Han Chinese and the Muslim Uighurs in 2009 and the continuing instability in the region, indeed forced Beijing to pay greater attention to the sources of international terrorism in Pakistan, given the prospect of Islamist extremism spilling over from Afghanistan and Pakistan into the restive autonomous region of western China. China's concerns about Islamist militancy on its western border have been rising, and the security environment in Afghanistan and the larger Central Asian region remains a huge worry. Yet, China refuses to discuss Pakistan with India in order to ensure that its privileged relationship with Pakistan remains intact, and US–China cooperation on Pakistan too has remained minimal.

China and India share a range of objectives in Pakistan, including preventing the rise and spread of extremism, fostering economic development in Afghanistan and Pakistan, overall political stability and social cohesion in Pakistan, and the safety of Pakistan's nuclear assets. Of all the major powers, it is China that can effectively leverage its growing economic profile in Pakistan to ensure that its security establishment cedes power to the civilians, allowing the state to function effectively. Chinese workers and assets have been targeted by extremists in Pakistan, and Chinese plans to emerge as a major investor in Afghanistan would remain a fantasy without Pakistan reining in extremist groups in Afghanistan.

The stability of the larger Central Asian region, crucial because of its oil and gas reserves, is also at stake. The major powers are keen to expand their influence in the region, and China is no exception. It shares many of the interests that other major powers, such as the US, Russia and India, have in Central Asia, including access to Central Asian energy resources, controlling the spread of radical Islam, ensuring political stability and strengthening regional economies. Continuing instability in Afghanistan and Pakistan poses a serious challenge to realizing these objectives. Yet, China's relationship with India has been very turbulent, impeding the realization of these and other mutual interests.[4]

With India's rise as an economic and political power of global significance, Sino-Indian ties are now at a critical juncture as India tries to find the right policy mix to deal with its most important neighbour. Meanwhile, Chinese strategists remain concerned about US attempts to encircle China and the profound effect on Chinese security of an eventual integration of India into a US alliance. China, according to this view, needs to remain vigilant against the growing network running 'from Japan to India' that would suffocate China.[5] As India struggles to emerge as a global power with an ambitious foreign policy agenda, China can effectively scuttle Indian ambitions by continuing with its diplomatic and military support to Pakistan. Much to India's chagrin, China periodically gives ample indications that it wants to follow that path.

With the Pakistani government under intense pressure from the US to do more to fight terrorism emanating from Pakistani soil, there are calls in Pakistan to adopt a foreign policy that considers China and not the US to be Pakistan's strongest ally and most significant stakeholder. China's emergence as a leading global economic power, coupled with attempts by India and the US to forge a closer relationship, has helped this suggestion gain further credibility. Washington has historically been accused of using Pakistan in times of need and then deserting it for a policy that favours stronger relations with India to serve the larger US strategic agenda. Pakistan remains angry about American indifference after the US used it to funnel aid to Afghan mujahideen and then turned its back on Pakistan after the Soviet withdrawal. Whereas only around 9 per cent of Pakistanis view the US as a partner, around 80 per cent of the Pakistani population considers China a friend.[6]

Though Beijing cannot replace Washington as an aid provider to Pakistan, the tension in US–Pakistan ties provides an opportunity for Beijing to deepen its relationship with Islamabad. As it is, China is considered a more reliable ally that has always come to Pakistan's aid when India has been on the rise, even to an extent that China has conveniently turned a blind eye to Pakistan's strategy of using terror as an instrument of policy against India. Not surprisingly, Pakistan declared in 2010 that it had given China a 'blank cheque' to intervene in India–Pakistan peace talks.[7] It also allowed Chinese engineers to examine the remains of the stealth helicopter destroyed during the raid that killed bin Laden—despite a direct request from the US that China not be allowed to do so.[8]

Suggestions emanating from Beijing that China might set up military bases overseas to counter US influence and exert pressure on India have been interpreted in certain sections in New Delhi as a veiled reference to China's interest in having a permanent military presence in Pakistan. Even though it might not be politically possible for the Pakistani government to follow through on such threats and openly allow China to set up a military base, New Delhi fears that Islamabad might allow Beijing use of Pakistani military facilities without any public announcement.[9] India is also concerned that China and Pakistan are coordinating their efforts in regard to border issues with India. The presence of the Chinese military in the Gilgit–Baltistan area of Pakistan Occupied Kashmir, purportedly to repair and upgrade the Karakoram Highway, has enormous implications for Indian security.[10]

China was the only major power that openly voiced support for Pakistan after bin Laden's assassination, defending Pakistan's role and underlining that the Pakistani government may not have known about bin Laden's presence in its territory. During then Pakistani Prime Minister Yousaf Raza Gilani's visit, China's then Premier Wen Jiabao affirmed that 'Pakistan has made huge sacrifices and an important contribution to the international fight against terrorism, that its independence, sovereignty, and territorial integrity must be respected, and that the international community should understand and support Pakistan's efforts to maintain domestic stability and to realize economic and social development'[11]. Wen went on to state that China would like to be an 'all-weather strategic partner' and would do its best to help the Pakistani government and people get through their difficulties.

Overall, it has been rightly observed that China's policy towards Pakistan is 'an object lesson in how to attain long-term national goals by calm calculation, forbearance, and diplomatic skill'[12]. Nevertheless, there are indeed limits to China–Pakistan ties. The relationship remains fundamentally asymmetrical: Pakistan wants more out of its ties with China than China is willing to offer. Given that Pakistan's domestic problems are gargantuan, China will be cautious about greater involvement. Moreover, the closer China gets to Pakistan, the faster India would move into the US orbit.

Meanwhile, the deteriorating internal security situation in Pakistan continues to strain Sino-Pakistan ties. The China Kingho Group, one of the country's largest private coal mining companies, pulled out in 2011 of what was to be Pakistan's largest foreign investment pact, citing concerns for the security of its personnel.[13] Amid worries about the potential destabilizing influence of Pakistani militants on China's Muslim minority in Xinjiang, Beijing has also taken a harder line against Pakistan. The flow of arms and terrorists from across the border in Pakistan remains a major headache for Chinese authorities, and Islamabad's inability and/or failure to curb extremism makes it difficult for the Chinese to trust Pakistan completely. If Pakistan wants to keep receiving support from China, it needs to demonstrate progress on this issue. As tensions rose between China and Pakistan in the aftermath of violence in the border town of Kashgar in Xinjiang in August 2011, then Pakistani President Zardari went to talk directly with local leaders and businessmen in Xinjiang, recognizing that if he was not able to mend fences with the local leadership, Sino-Pakistan ties would be in real jeopardy.

China, at least publicly, emphasized that its relationship with Pakistan is far more important than isolated incidents of violence. Flirtation with Pakistan gives China crucial space for diplomatic manoeuvring vis-à-vis India and the US, and it will continue to utilize the relationship in pursuit of its larger strategic objectives. Pakistan will not be a common interest that binds China with either India or the US. But with Western forces leaving Afghanistan, there is a new urgency in China's Afghanistan policy.

In September 2012, China's then security chief Zhou Yongkang became the first senior Chinese leader to visit Afghanistan in almost five decades. With this visit, Beijing signalled an end to its policy of 'masterful inactivity' vis-à-vis Kabul. During Zhou's visit, Beijing announced a pact 'to train, fund, and equip Afghan police', underscoring China's growing interest in Afghanistan's internal security affairs. China also started holding trilateral consultations with Pakistan and Afghanistan on regional security. Much like the rest of the region, China was worried about the withdrawal of Western forces from Afghanistan as it feared a broader destabilization after 2014. The growing problems in Pakistan also alerted China to the reality that its leverage over Pakistan may not be enough in managing the regional turmoil. As tensions rose in Xinjiang, the perceived Pakistan link to Uighur militancy led to a reassessment of China's approach to Afghanistan, especially as concerns rose in Beijing that Islamabad was not very effective in controlling the training of Uighur militants in Pakistan.

Since 2001, China had adopted a hands-off policy towards Afghanistan, preferring the US to do most of the heavy lifting. It did not want a serious involvement in Afghanistan but it also did not want a victory for the extremists, given its negative impact on China's problems with Uighur separatists in Xinjiang. Apart from the $3 billion Aynak copper mine project, China also did not make a significant attempt to project its economic power in Afghanistan. But as the departure of Western forces from Afghanistan approached, China upped its game in Afghanistan. It was in 2007 that the state-owned China Metallurgical Group Corporation secured a thirty-year lease on MesAynak in Afghanistan's Logar province. Though progress was slow and Afghan insurgents targeted the mine, Beijing expected to extract $100 billion worth of copper from the site. The China National Petroleum Corporation (CNPC) also helped Afghanistan in setting up the country's first commercial oil production site, which was likely to extract 1.5 million barrels of oil annually from 2013.[14]

China's humongous appetite for resources will make sure that Afghanistan, with over $1 trillion in potential mineral wealth, gets adequate attention from Beijing. With China's backing, Afghanistan became an observer in the SCO, and China signed a strategic partnership agreement with Kabul in 2012. More significantly, Beijing has access to the Taliban through Pakistan, having been the only non-Islamic nation in touch with Mullah Omar in the late 1990s. Viewing a political settlement in Afghanistan as increasingly important for protecting its economic and security interests in the region, Beijing has been quietly expanding its links with the Taliban and seeking assurances that its interests would be secure if the Taliban were to come back to power.[15] It remains far from clear if Beijing would be able to utilize Afghan resources for its economic sustenance without incurring significant costs as Afghanistan's security environment unravels post 2014.

RUSSIA FORGES NEW ALIGNMENTS

In an attempt to broaden its strategic space after the withdrawal of Western forces from Afghanistan post 2014, Pakistan also made an attempt to reach out to Russia. Pakistan's then President Zardari visited Russia in May 2012, and the Russian president's special envoy for Afghanistan Zamir Kabulov visited Pakistan the following month. Pakistan's then army chief General Ashfaq Parvez Kayani visited Russia in October 2012 in a renewed attempt to improve relations with Moscow. His visit came after the cancellation of the visit of Russian President Vladimir Putin to Pakistan. This would have been the first ever visit of a Russian president to Pakistan and, as such, was loaded with significance. Putin was also to participate in a quadrilateral meeting on Afghanistan with leaders of Tajikistan, Pakistan and Afghanistan. In place of Putin, his foreign minister was sent to Pakistan.

Both countries are also trying to increase their presence in Central Asia. Russia wants stability in its Central Asian periphery, and Pakistan remains critical in managing the region. Moscow's outreach to Islamabad is an attempt to get a handle on this regional dynamic. Russia has taken note of Indian foreign policy's changing priorities and the downturn in US–Pakistan ties. The US–India rapprochement has been problematic for Russia. As India moves away from Russia, especially as its dependence on defence equipment decreases, Moscow is also looking for alternatives. Moscow also recognizes the importance of Pakistan in restoring stability to a post-2014 Afghanistan and the larger Central

Asian region. So there are various factors at work here in this outreach. It was Putin who had publicly endorsed Pakistan's bid to join the SCO and had offered Russian help in managing Pakistan's energy infrastructure. He went on to suggest that Russia views Pakistan as a reliable and very important partner.

Russia's Gazprom wants to invest in the Turkmenistan–Afghanistan–Pakistan–India gas pipeline. Meanwhile, though Russia has been one of the biggest beneficiaries of the externalities from the Indo-US civilian nuclear energy cooperation pact—with two nuclear reactors at the Kudankulam power plant being Russian and pacts for two more having been signed—there have been rumblings in Moscow regarding the manner in which the project has been handled by New Delhi, leading to severe delays, and because of the civil nuclear liability law of India, which makes India an unattractive market for the Russian nuclear sector.

After deciding to ignore Pakistan for decades in its arms sales matrix, Moscow has now decided to gradually start weapons sales to Pakistan. Russia is the world's second largest arms exporter, with a 24 per cent share of the trade, surpassed only by the US, which controls almost 30 per cent of the global arms market. India continues to account for over 50 per cent of Russian arms sales, but New Delhi has diversified its suppliers.

As the arms market becomes a difficult place for Russia to navigate, with China deciding to produce its own weapons rather than procuring them from Russia, Moscow needs new buyers. India's move away from Russia has been gradual but significant. The Medium Multi-Role Combat Aircraft deal with French Rafale was as as big a setback to Russia as it was to the US. In a far-reaching decision for Russia and India as well as the broader South Asian strategic landscape, Russia decided in June 2014 to lift an embargo on supplying weapons and military hardware to Pakistan. Sergey Chemezov, head of Russian state-run technologies corporation Rostec, suggested that Moscow was negotiating the delivery of several Mi-25 helicopter gunships to Islamabad. Moscow's ambassador to India, Alexander M. Kadakin, tried to justify this to India by suggesting that Russia had never imposed any arms embargo on Pakistan and that its technical and military cooperation with the country dated back to the 1960s. Defence sales to Pakistan could open up a potentially new and open-ended market for Russia as the appetite in Washington to sustain Pakistan's military-industrial complex declines dramatically. Defence cooperation as envisaged by the two sides may involve joint military exercises, exchange of personnel and defence sales.

But there are clear limits here. Moscow can never substitute for Washington as far as aid and defence support to Pakistan is concerned. It is severely constrained in what it can do, and Pakistan's needs are huge. It is unlikely that Russia will emerge as a major benefactor, but Pakistan wants to show the US that it has other options. In the past, Moscow was very critical of the Pakistani military establishment's propensity to use extremist groups to further their nation's strategic ends. And it remains worried about this tendency, so the pressure on Pakistan will continue.

The Russian establishment also feels strongly about the possibility of nuclear technology falling into the hands of extremists in Pakistan and has been very vocal about this threat. Nor would Moscow like to share its defence technology with Pakistan to the extent that it alienates India, one of its largest markets for defence equipment. Russia deals with India on a number of levels, but their partnership could be jeopardized if Pakistan becomes a major priority for Moscow.

Whatever shape Russia–Pakistan ties take eventually, the fact that Moscow is reaching out to Pakistan and shaping new alignments in South Asia exemplifies Pakistan's centrality amidst a regional flux and how most regional states are now trying to hedge their bets in an ever evolving strategic environment.

Pakistan and Iran Slug It Out

Though most consider the India–Pakistan rivalry to be at the heart of the Afghanistan conundrum, the other regional rivalry that has been played out in Afghanistan is between Pakistan and Iran. This rivalry has a long pedigree. Pakistan became the transit point for weapons and aid to Saudi-funded, US-equipped, and Pakistani-trained mujahideen who fought to drive the Red Army from Afghanistan. Pakistani authorities, however, put a filter on the aid. The loss of Bangladesh—formerly East Pakistan—in 1971 had led the Pakistani leadership to be very wary of ethnic nationalism. Pashtun nationalism in Afghanistan had challenged Pakistani cohesion for as long as Bengali nationalism. The Pakistani government, therefore, only allowed aid to flow to those groups who rallied around a sectarian rather than a nationalist identity.

The Iranian authorities, in contrast, miscalculated. While generous with aid to their allies, they had far fewer resources at their disposal because of the ongoing war of attrition with Iraq. That aid which Iranian officials could provide, they limited largely to Shiite and ethnic Farsi-speaking Tajik groups. This transformed a potential Afghanistan-wide influence into a far more localized interest. Nor, in contrast to the actions of the Pakistani leadership, did Iranian authorities properly cultivate or manage their population of Afghan refugees in order to spread their influence. Tehran did not want to cede the advantage to Islamabad, though, and continued to fight for influence in Afghanistan, even as the Pakistan- and Saudi-backed Taliban consolidated control over 90 per cent of the country. This proxy fight, however, polarized Afghanistan and brewed further Pakistan–Iran mistrust.

The terrorist attacks of 9/11 changed the foreign policy priorities of both Iran and Pakistan. The George W. Bush administration's tough stance forced then President Pervez Musharraf to support Washington's 'war on terror', which ended Taliban rule in Kabul. Though Iranian officials welcomed the move, they soon found themselves encircled by US forces in Pakistan, Afghanistan, Central Asia and the Persian Gulf.

While Karzai's government has been nominally supported by both Tehran and Islamabad, neither neighbour has been willing to sacrifice its own interests. With time, tension has increased. Iran retains its special interests in Afghanistan's western Herat region, until 1857 part of Iran, and Pakistan considers the Pashto-speaking southern sections of Afghanistan to be within its sphere of influence.

Kabul remains a contested area within that sphere. The deterioration in Afghan security, perhaps sparked by one or both, has also created a dynamic of increasing tension between Iran and Pakistan. Increasingly, as a perception of US weakness spreads, Iran has raised its rhetoric against the presence of US and NATO troops in Afghanistan, which Islamabad nominally supports, at least publicly. Tehran continues to blame the US presence in Afghanistan for continuing instability in the region.

Notwithstanding some tentative attempts by Pakistan and Iran to improve their bilateral ties, the two countries' relationship remains strained. Rather than bringing the two states together, the situation in Afghanistan has provided a stage where their rivalry is once again played out. Though the vacuum resulting from the fall of the Taliban government is the main factor behind the rising turmoil in Afghanistan, the problem there also remains a regional one. The more the US and its NATO allies fail to secure Afghanistan, the more neighbouring states will revive their ties to ethnic and ideological proxies, creating a dynamic that will further undermine Afghanistan. While both Pakistan and Iran seem to have concluded that a stable, independent and economically strong Afghan state is preferable to a weak and troubled one, they remain very sensitive to their relative gains vis-à-vis each other. Regardless of who runs Afghanistan, Tehran's and Islamabad's conflicting interests over Afghanistan have played a pivotal role in the formation of their foreign policies towards each other.

Iran's growing ties with India also cloud its relationship with Pakistan. During the early phase of the Cold War,

Tehran had supported Pakistan because it was resisting Nasserism, the Arab nationalist political ideology, in the region. It, therefore, tried to cultivate an ally in Pakistan by providing it direct military assistance during the 1965 war with India and sided with Islamabad in the 1971 war. However, that kind of trust between Iran and Pakistan has now disappeared. Though Pakistan is not seen as an adversary of Iran even now, the Sunni fundamentalism of jihadi variety considers the 20 per cent Shia population of Pakistan as apostates. This is the same variant of Islamist fundamentalism that supports and sends jihadi terrorists to India.

There was also a perception shared by India and Iran that Pakistan's control of Afghanistan via the fundamentalist Taliban regime was not in the strategic interests of either state and was a threat to the regional stability of the entire region.[16] As opposed to Pakistan, which promptly recognized the Taliban regime,[17] India and Iran did not establish diplomatic contacts with the Taliban.[18] India and Iran, together with Russia, were the main supporters of the anti-Taliban Northern Alliance that routed the hard-line Islamic regime with US help in Afghanistan in November 2001.

India's ability to cultivate ties with Iran and Afghanistan leaves Pakistan vulnerable as it finds itself surrounded by states with a distinct anti-Pakistan orientation. Pakistan remains concerned about deepening India–Iran ties and Afghanistan's gravitation towards such an axis.[19] For many in Pakistan, India is pursuing a well-crafted strategy of encircling Pakistan and keeping it out of Afghanistan and Central Asia altogether. This seems an exaggerated assessment of Indian foreign policy towards the region in general and towards Iran in particular. Though there's hardly anything 'strategic' in India's relationship with Iran, any step by India and Iran towards cooperation is fraught with trouble for Pakistan.[20]

Historically, Iran and Pakistan have competed for influence in Afghanistan, and Iran has had to suffer the consequences of Pakistan's attempts at establishing and supporting a fundamentalist Sunni regime in Kabul. Iran's dissatisfaction with Pakistan flows from Islamabad's military ties with the US and close economic and cultural ties to Saudi Arabia. Deterioration in the security situation in Afghanistan has once again brought tensions between Iran and Pakistan to the fore.[21] Iran's internal cohesion and external security have come under strain with the growing instability in Afghanistan and Pakistan.

The collapse of the Afghan state's authority is increasing Iran's own insecurity by creating a massive influx of drugs and weapons. The spectre of Afghanistan's ethnic conflict has threatened to spill into Iran along with the economic burdens of supporting millions of Afghan refugees. A refugee crisis is emerging in Iran with 2,000 to 4,000 refugees entering Iran every day from Afghanistan, according to some estimates.[22] Iran lacks the socio-economic infrastructure to absorb the flow of refugees in such a large number. Given the absence of Western aid, it has found it difficult to deal with this crisis effectively. It is not surprising, therefore, that reports have emerged of Iran forcibly deporting up to 2,000 Afghan refugees per day, many of whom had lived in Iran for many years.[23]

The failure to wean Afghanistan away from poppy cultivation has led to Iran emerging as a transit route for narcotics into West Asia and Europe. This has resulted in an escalation of violence in Iran's Sistan and Baluchistan province, further aggravating tensions along the Iran–Pakistan border. Though Iran has taken a proactive stance against drug smuggling, it has found it difficult to tackle this challenge due to its porous borders with Pakistan and Afghanistan. In May 2008, Afghanistan, Iran and Pakistan agreed on a triangular initiative to cooperate more closely in counter-narcotics efforts, including through the establishment of a joint cell, to be located in Tehran, which will facilitate information exchange and joint counter-narcotics interventions. It has failed to have any perceptible influence on the narcotics trade so far.

Iran has been increasing its influence in Afghanistan, using its oil money to realize its self-image as an ascendant regional power. Iran's strategy towards Afghanistan seems geared towards hastening the withdrawal of American forces, preventing the Taliban from gaining power, and trying to keep Afghanistan under Tehran's sway. It played a major role in restarting the post-Taliban political process in Afghanistan and has pledged $560 million in aid and loans to Afghanistan.[24] But Iran's role has become more complicated in Afghanistan. The perception that other states such as Pakistan, Saudi Arabia and in particular the US would gain an upper hand in the evolving political environment in Afghanistan has pushed Iran into charting a proactive course towards its eastern neighbour. There are indications that certain sections of the Iranian military may be arming the Taliban to weaken the American military in Afghanistan. Time and again, the US and NATO forces have intercepted shipments of weapons being supplied to the Taliban that seem to have originated in Iran.[25] There is little common ground between Iran and Pakistan on a solution to the Afghan crisis, and history seems to be repeating itself with both states once again funding proxy wars between Shias and Sunnis in each other's countries as well as in Afghanistan, increasing the likelihood of a major sectarian explosion in the region.[26]

Iran has learnt from its past experience in Afghanistan. It doesn't want to give Pakistan a free hand, and so it is exploiting the opportunities presented to it by the new political dispensation in Afghanistan and spreading its influence. Iran has tried to project itself as a responsible regional actor since the fall of the Taliban in 2001, urging the Northern Alliance to accept the Bonn agreement for the formation of a new broad-based government in Kabul and offering aid and loans as well as training Afghan soldiers. It is heavily investing in construction projects in the western parts of Afghanistan, building roads, rail links and border posts. However, other interests are also at play, with Iran using this unprecedented opportunity to support conservative Shia religious schools and warlords as well as increasing its intelligence activities across Afghanistan. Iran has viewed itself traditionally as the guarantor of the security of Afghanistan's Shiites, who are around 20 per cent of the whole nation. Iran would like US forces to leave Afghanistan, and, if possible, hasten their withdrawal while keeping the Taliban at bay even as it would like to ensure that western Afghanistan remains under its influence.

Several media reports from Afghanistan suggest that Iran has been increasing its operations in Afghanistan in an effort to gain influence with the contending insurgent factions and to hasten the departure of US troops from the country.[27] Unlike in the 1990s, when Iran unequivocally opposed the Taliban regime in Afghanistan, with the Revolutionary Guards supporting one of the only anti-Taliban resistance movements in western Afghanistan that was able to continue fighting the regime until 2001, Iran now seems ready to cooperate with and support any group, regardless of its religion and language, which can fight the US presence in Afghanistan.[28] Not only has the Taliban opened an office in the Iranian city of Zahedan but the Revolutionary Guards has also been considering sending surface-to-air missiles to insurgents in Afghanistan.

Growing tensions between Afghanistan and Pakistan are also working to Iran's advantage, with Kabul increasingly dependent on Iran for its transit trade routes. The Karzai government cannot pick fights with both its vital neighbours and so is trying to keep Iran in good humour. While the US maintains that Iran is funnelling weapons into Afghanistan, the Afghan government continues to view Iran as a close friend and ally.[29] Meanwhile, Iran, facing US and NATO troops in Afghanistan, has an interest in striking US forces and helping to push them from the region by supplying insurgents in both countries with funds, weapons, and training. Tehran warned in 2012 that the Washington–Kabul pact that allowed American troops to stay in Afghanistan beyond 2014 'will intensify insecurity and instability in Afghanistan'. It even tried to put pressure on Afghanistan to scuttle the strategic partnership agreement with the US, threatening to deport Afghan refugees and migrant workers if Afghanistan's parliament ratified the deal.[30]

The Obama administration's decision to leave Afghanistan beginning 2014 has left the field open for Pakistan. Karzai's interest in reconciling elements of the Taliban leadership is generating apprehensions in Iran. Because of Taliban's historic ties to Pakistan's intelligence and military, for Iran such a move would give Pakistan new influence in Afghanistan. Iran remains worried about any greater political role for leaders of the almost exclusively Sunni Taliban. Iran has encouraged India to send more of its assistance to provinces in northern and western Afghanistan that are under the control of those associated with the anti-Taliban Northern Alliance.[31] New possibilities have opened up in India–Iran ties as well as in the Iran–Afghanistan relationship with the emergence of a US–Iran rapprochement under the new Iranian leadership of President Hassan Rouhani. It remains to be seen, however, if this will have a substantive impact on the ground realities in Afghanistan.

Iran will only play a positive role in Afghanistan if it feels its vital interests are not under threat, and a deteriorating security environment in Afghanistan will only make Iran feel more vulnerable, forcing it to take steps to safeguard its interests, letting the conflict spiral further. Pakistan, meanwhile, is reluctant to cede the pre-eminent position it has enjoyed for the last several decades in determining Afghanistan's political trajectory. And as the security environment in Afghanistan deteriorates further, Islamabad will view this as an opportunity to maintain its presence in its neighbour's territory in order to secure its larger strategic interests.

PAKISTAN'S DANGEROUS GAME

As the dust settled in the aftermath of bin Laden's death at the hands of US special forces in May 2011, it was clear that either the Pakistani state was in league with the Al Qaeda or it was so weak and incompetent that it was not able to control rogue elements within its structures.[32] Bin Laden, the world's most-wanted fugitive, was found living in the heart of Abbottabad—within commuting distance of Islamabad—just a week after then Pakistani army chief Kayani, during his visit to the military academy in the same town, had declared that his troops had 'broken the backs' of militants. Pakistan's failure to locate bin Laden, and the unilateral US decision to capture and kill him, led to allegations of complicity and incompetence in Pakistan. The security establishment and the ISI in particular came in for rare and sustained public criticism, forcing its head, Lieutenant General Ahmed Shuja Pasha, to offer his resignation after admitting to an intelligence failure.

It was indeed ironic then, when five days after the Abbottabad raid, Kayani demanded that the number of American forces in the country be reduced 'to the minimum essential' and that any similar American action ought to warrant a 'review' of the whole relationship between the two countries.[33] The civilian authorities too tried their best to shield the security services. Declaring that 'this was an intelligence failure of the whole world, not Pakistan alone', then Prime Minister Gilani absolved the army and the ISI of 'either complicity or incompetence'[34]. The Pakistani army had long been viewed as one institution that could keep a nation beset by militancy and weak civilian governments intact. The US raid that killed bin Laden, however, raised profound questions about the very credibility of the army and whether the assurances provided by it, including the one about the security of its nuclear arsenal, could be trusted.[35]

Despite receiving massive aid from the US, which also virtually underwrote its military expansion, Pakistan is one of the most anti-American countries in the world and an economic basket case. The Pakistani security establishment openly supported the Taliban until 11 September 2001, and since then, despite official disavowal, support has continued. So long as Pakistan continues to harbour and support the Taliban and other extremist groups, Afghanistan won't be able to achieve lasting stability.

The consequences of its short-sighted policies are there for all to see: an unstable Afghanistan and a Pakistan on the verge of a breakdown. The nation is under attack, but the wounds are self-inflicted. Despite the rhetoric, India is not the biggest danger Pakistan faces. It is the extremist groups that the security establishment nurtured over the years that have turned against the Pakistani state. The Pakistani army has yet to reconcile itself to the idea that Afghanistan should be something other than its strategic backyard, under the control of its proxies such as the Taliban, and continues to struggle with its paranoia that India is encroaching on Afghanistan to encircle its old enemy. It remains angry with the US for abandoning it after the Afghan jihad and for sanctioning it over the nuclear programme.

Washington's frustration at its inability to persuade the Pakistani army and intelligence apparatus to cease supporting the Afghan Taliban and other militants is also palpable. It is clear from the WikiLeaks documents that Washington remains convinced Pakistan will never cooperate fully in fighting the whole range of extremist groups. It is also well understood in the US that Pakistan is preparing for the eventual American withdrawal from Afghanistan, viewing the militant groups as an insurance and as a means of exerting influence inside Afghanistan and against India.

The assessment of a former US ambassador, Anne Patterson, is blunt: 'There is no chance that Pakistan will view enhanced assistance levels in any field as sufficient compensation for abandoning support for these groups, which it sees as an important part of its national security apparatus against India.' The burgeoning US–India ties, she says, 'feeds Pakistani establishment paranoia and pushes [it] closer to both Afghan- and Kashmir-focused terrorist groups'[36]. Former US Secretary of State Hillary Clinton was also unequivocal in her assertion in 2011 that despite public disavowals, 'some officials of Pakistan's Inter-Services Intelligence Directorate continue to maintain ties with a wide array of extremist organizations', in particular the Taliban and the LeT.[37] After receiving nearly $20 billion in direct aid from the US over the last decade, the Pakistani army is not shy of playing hardball, convinced that it is America that needs Pakistan, not the other way round.

The Pakistani army has refused to make any move against the Quetta Shura, the operational nerve centre in Pakistan of Taliban leader Mullah Omar. Groups like the LeT and Sipah-e-Sihaba Pakistan continue to operate openly, despite being nominally banned. CIA drone strikes have been largely limited to Pakistan's FATA, as the Pakistani government has not allowed any strikes in Baluchistan where senior Taliban leadership is believed to be hiding. The international community wants the Pakistani military to act against Mullah Omar, the Haqqani Network and the LeT. Yet these groups are viewed as long-standing assets of the Pakistani army and intelligence. The LeT is now a potent threat to the West. Its leader, Hafiz Muhammad Saeed, who is wanted for his role in the Mumbai attacks, openly proclaimed in 2011 that bin Laden 'was a great person who awakened the Muslim world'[38].

The assassination of Burhanuddin Rabbani, Afghanistan's former president and principal negotiator for talks with the Taliban, as well as terrorist assaults targeting the US embassy and NATO headquarters in Kabul in September 2011, further aggravated tensions between the two allies. The US blamed the Haqqani Network for the coordinated attacks. Despite being pressed, the Pakistani security establishment remains reluctant to take on the Haqqani Network in North Waziristan. The Haqqani group is an important player in the emerging security dynamic in Afghanistan, and the Pakistani military views it as an important asset in countering Indian influence in Afghanistan. Not surprisingly, Kayani even offered to help broker a deal between the Haqqani group and the Afghan government.

Pakistan remains adamant about underlining its centrality in the unfolding endgame in Afghanistan, making it clear time and again that only Islamabad and Rawalpindi can bring the Afghan Taliban into the political mainstream. The Pakistani army wants to retain its central role in mediation efforts at all costs. It matters little if in the process the very foundation of the Pakistani state has eroded away.

One of the ways in which Pakistan has been able to blackmail the international community is by underlining the grave implications of a failed nuclear state. Growing radicalization of the security forces is a potent challenge, raising questions about the safety of Pakistan's nuclear installations. Pakistan's government continues to dismiss media reports that its nuclear weapons were in danger of falling into the wrong hands as 'inspired'. It continues to stress that Pakistan has provided the highest level of institutionalized protection to its strategic assets. Nonetheless, the credibility of such claims remains open to question. Instituted in 2000, Pakistan's nuclear command and control arrangements are centred on the National Command Authority, which comprises the Employment Control Committee, the Development Control Committee, and the Strategic Plans Division. Only a small group of military officials apparently have access to the country's nuclear assets.

It is instructive to note that of all the major nuclear states in world, Pakistan is the only country where the nuclear button is in the hands of the military. Moreover, senior civilian and military officials responsible for these weapons have a problematic track record of maintaining close control over them. A.Q. Khan was the head of the Pakistani nuclear programme—and a veritable national hero—but was instrumental in making Pakistan the centre of the biggest nuclear proliferation network by leaking technology to states far and wide, including Iran, North

Korea and Libya. Pakistani nuclear scientists have even travelled to Afghanistan at the behest of bin Laden.

According to US intelligence estimates, Pakistan's nuclear arsenal now totals more than 100 deployed weapons. It is ahead of India in the production of uranium and plutonium for bombs and development of delivery weapons. It is producing nuclear weapons at a faster rate than any other country in the world. It will soon be the world's fourth largest nuclear weapon state ahead of France and Britain and behind only the US, Russia and China.[39] It has not only acquired plutonium capability with Chinese help but is also working towards miniaturizing its nuclear warheads. The rapid expansion of its nuclear arsenal has largely come in the form of new, smaller, more mobile weapons that are easier to steal. Also, a number of attacks on Pakistani military installations, including the general headquarters of the Pakistan army in Rawalpindi in 2009, the naval base PNS *Mehran* in Karachi in 2011, and the Kamra airbase in 2012, have compounded the anxiety of the world about its nuclear programme. It has tried to reassure the world that its arsenal is safe and secure, and a 2008 US Congressional report noted that the weapons were stored in secure underground facilities, unassembled, and separate from their launchers.[40]

Yet the problem of growing radicalization in the Pakistani military's rank and file cannot be underestimated. Documents released by WikiLeaks underscore this problem. The Pakistani air force reportedly admitted to radicalization in its ranks when it detailed acts of sabotage against its F-16 aircraft to prevent their deployment in support of operations against Taliban militants in FATA.[41] Some have even suggested that Washington has made a tacit agreement with Islamabad according to which the US will leave Pakistan's nuclear programme alone in exchange for cooperation on Afghanistan.[42] Washington has pushed Pakistan since 2007 to accept help in moving highly enriched uranium out of an ageing Pakistani nuclear reactor, fearing it could be diverted for illicit purposes.

In May 2009, then US ambassador to Pakistan Anne Patterson reported that Pakistan had refused to allow American experts to visit the site, and cited concerns expressed by a Pakistani official that 'if the local media got word of the fuel removal, they certainly would portray it as the US taking Pakistan's nuclear weapons'[43]. She wrote in a separate document that 'our major concern is not having an Islamic militant steal an entire weapon but rather the chance someone working in GOP [government of Pakistan] facilities could gradually smuggle enough material out to eventually make a weapon'[44]. It is this fear that Pakistan has been effectively able to leverage in its ties with the West and the US in particular.

The Afghan endeavour will fail if the US does not find a way to eliminate the de facto sanctuary that Taliban fighters have established in Pakistan. This is now well recognized by American officials in Afghanistan.[45] In a major departure from the long-standing US policy of publicly playing down Pakistan's official support for insurgents operating from havens within Pakistan, Admiral Mike Mullen, former chairman of the US Joint Chiefs of Staff and a strong supporter of close ties with the Pakistani military, described the Haqqani Network as a 'veritable arm' of Pakistan's ISI in 2011.[46] This was a signal from Washington that it would no longer tolerate continuing use of terrorist groups, aided and abetted by the ISI, to kill Americans and their allies in Afghanistan.

Pakistan's sponsorship of the Haqqani Network has long been an open secret, as has been the reality that Haqqanis have been responsible for some of the most murderous assaults on Indian and Western presence in Afghanistan. In response to America's increasingly vocal protests, Islamabad was quick to signal publicly that it was prepared to lean away from Washington. Yet major powers with interest in Central Asia, including China, do not have much sympathy for Pakistan's desire to strengthen radical Sunni groups. China is as interested as the US and India in effective Pakistani action against the terror sanctuaries in North Waziristan.

The transactional relationship that the US has constructed with Pakistan over the last several decades is likely to continue in the near future, despite growing strategic divergences between the two. America needs Pakistan in order to get precious supplies to Afghanistan, mainly via the Pakistani port of Karachi, and American policymakers remain wary of isolating a country with one of the fastest growing nuclear arsenals. At the same time, the Pakistani military has continued to offer just enough cooperation to keep the billions of dollars of American aid flowing. The US–Pakistan ties hit their nadir in 2011 when a series of events led to widespread disaffection on both sides. These included the killing of two Pakistani assailants by a security officer of the US Central Intelligence Agency, the raid in Abbottabad that killed bin Laden and led to charges of violations of Pakistani sovereignty, and an American airstrike on a Pakistani border outpost killing twenty-four soldiers. Pakistan continues to blackmail the US by underlining instability to make the withdrawal of Western forces from Afghanistan messy and difficult. This was once again reflected in Hillary Clinton's September 2012 decision to set aside legal restrictions that would have blocked $2 billion in US economic and military assistance.[47]

Yet American and Pakistani interests are likely to diverge much more radically as the US exit from Afghanistan draws closer. Regional instability will continue to be the norm in South Asia unless Pakistan's double dealing is exposed fully and strong regional pressure against its meddling in Afghan politics is built. Pakistan is at war with itself as well as with the rest of the world. Unless Pakistan's military–jihadi complex is completely dismantled, it will continue to pose a threat to the world. The biggest challenge comes from the rapid ascendancy of the Pakistani military in the nation's power structure and, as a corollary, in shaping Pakistan's strategic agenda. Instead of helping the civilian government get traction, Washington itself has pulled the rug from under its doddering feet. By relying on the Pakistani military to secure its short-term ends in Afghanistan, the US has made sure that the fundamental malaise afflicting Pakistan—the militarization of the Pakistani state—will continue to afflict Pakistan and South Asia with grave implications for sustainable long-term peace in the subcontinent.

It is important for the US to recognize that it is not the only player in the sandpit, nor is its struggle to stabilize the Karzai regime and battle the Taliban the only fight going on in the country. Indeed, unless there is a fundamental change in the attitudes of regional powers, Afghanistan will remain a battleground—if not for armies, then for their proxies.

Conflicting interests over Afghanistan have tended to play a pivotal role in the formation of foreign policies of regional powers vis-à-vis each other, and that continues to be the case. Afghanistan's predicament is a difficult one. It would like to enhance its links with its neighbouring states so as to gain economic advantages and tackle common threats to regional security. Yet, such interactions also leave it open to becoming a theatre for the neighbouring states where they can play out their regional rivalries. Peace and stability will continue to elude Afghanistan so long as its neighbours continue to view it through the lens of their regional rivalries and as a chessboard for enhancing their regional power and influence. And these regional rivalries will only intensify if the perception gains ground that the security situation in Afghanistan is deteriorating. This is the dilemma that confronts America as it begins its exit from Afghanistan in 2014 and also India which will have to bear the brunt of the changing regional realities.

CHAPTER 6

THE US–INDIA–AFGHAN MATRIX: CONFUSED SIGNALS, DISASTROUS CONSEQUENCES

'A decade ago, the BJP government wanted to help us militarily but we refused due to Pakistan's sensitivities. This time, we are keen but India is hesitant.'

—Zalmai Rassoul, Afghan foreign minister, in May 2013

Obama's Exit Gambit

STABILIZING AFGHANISTAN EMERGED AS THE topmost foreign policy priority of the Obama administration, and, soon after assuming office, it announced a new policy towards the Af–Pak region. From India's perspective, two aspects of the policy stood out. One involved differentiating between a 'good' Taliban and a 'bad' Taliban, as discussed in Chapter 2.

The second strand of the strategy was a growing focus on Pakistan, with an increasing realization that the real source of the problems in Afghanistan was the Afghan–Pakistan border area where most of the Al Qaeda leadership had relocated after being shunted out of Afghanistan. Towards this end, greater financial and military aid was to be provided to Pakistan to enable it to focus more on strengthening its counter-insurgency capabilities in order to fight more effectively with the extremists. The Biden–Lugar Bill, called the Enhanced Partnership with Pakistan Bill, was reintroduced in the senate in 2009 as the Kerry–Lugar Bill, leading to a quantum jump in aid to Pakistan, tripling the US non-military assistance to an annual $1.5 billion while continuing the military aid of the Bush administration.

For the US and the NATO, tired as they were of their Afghan venture, such an approach made it possible to think of departing from the region over the next three to four years. However, the way the US went about delineating its strategy made it highly unlikely that the strategy would work. It was more likely to provoke a much more fierce regional competition leading to greater regional instability.

The idea that the US could do business with the Taliban was not new. This was what had led the administration of former US President Bill Clinton (1992–2000) to turn a blind eye to Taliban's rise to power in Kabul and its medieval practices, all in the name of good old-fashioned realism. Though former Pakistan President Musharraf committed Pakistan to support efforts to stabilize Afghanistan after the fall of the Taliban and agreed to strengthen the Karzai administration, doubts never ceased as to Islamabad's capacity and commitment to crack down on terrorists and militants. The rejuvenation of the Taliban bolstered Pakistan's role as a front-line state in the war on terrorism, securing often lucrative assistance from the US. The ISI and Pakistani military elite also see Pakistan engaged in a proxy war for influence in Afghanistan. The Taliban may be a concern to both Kabul and Washington, but Islamabad has been more than willing to tolerate jihadist violence so long as it is focused on Afghanistan, Kashmir or other parts of India.

There is no 'moderate' Taliban in as much as there is no 'radical' Taliban. The goal of various factions is the same even though their strategies might differ on the surface. It is chimerical to assume that the US can negotiate its way out of the mess by luring the 'moderate' Taliban. The Taliban are not amenable to a reasonable political bargain in Afghanistan as their primary aim is to restructure the Afghan state to smoothen their own passage to power in Kabul.

The other strand of Obama's strategy—that of reorienting the American foreign policy to Pakistan—was undermined by a lack of awareness of regional balance of power sensitivities. The idea in Western capitals that India could somehow be persuaded to negotiate with Pakistan on Kashmir, allowing the Pakistani government to concentrate less on its feud with India and more on its turbulent western frontier, looked good only on paper. India and Pakistan were close to a deal on Kashmir in 2007 not because of any outside pressure but because India was confident of the support of the friendlier Bush administration. The Obama administration's clumsy handling of India in its early years in office put India once again on the defensive, and a defensive India was never going to give the US what it wanted most.

It was indeed remarkable how quickly goodwill towards the US disappeared in New Delhi. Small signals emanating from Washington had a much bigger impact in the corridors of power in India than perhaps intended. It was instructive that the only context in which Obama talked of India in his early days was the need to sort Kashmir out so as to find a way out for the West's troubles in Afghanistan. The talk of a strategic partnership between the two democracies all but disappeared.

Former Secretary of State Hillary Clinton's omission of India as part of her first trip to Asia; her assertion that the US–China bilateral relationship was the most important one in the world; the appointment of Jeff Bader, a China expert, as the senior director of East Asia who was to be looking at India; the US reluctance to make India part of its larger strategy towards the region despite sharing a common interest in tackling terrorism and extremism from the turbulent territory between the Indus and the Hindu Kush— all pointed to a dramatic re-calibration in the US approach towards India. There was a growing sense in New Delhi that India would have to formulate its own strategy vis-à-vis its neighbourhood, devoid of any unrealistic expectations from Washington.

The Obama administration, meanwhile, also suggested that Karzai bore considerable responsibility for all that had been going wrong in Afghanistan, refusing to root out corruption and preferring cronies to competent managers. The American civilian leadership lost all faith in Karzai and vice versa. More damagingly for the Obama administration, the views of the American civilian leadership did not align closely with those of the then top American military commander in Afghanistan, General Stanley McChrystal. Obama himself didn't help his cause when he started publicly rebuking Karzai for various governance failures in Afghanistan. True, Karzai had spectacularly failed in constructing modern governmental machinery and seemed to have little interest in building provincial and local governance institutions. But, for better or for worse, that was the hand that Washington had been dealt in Afghanistan. It made no sense to alienate him at a crucial time when discussions on the eventual departure of Western forces from Afghanistan were beginning to take place. But that's exactly what happened, making a bad situation worse.

There were growing tensions within the Obama administration over the size and pace of the planned pullout of US troops from Afghanistan, with the military seeking to limit a reduction in combat forces and the White House pressing for a withdrawal substantial enough to placate a war-weary electorate. At a time of economic turmoil in the US, the war's cost had led to increasing public disenchantment with it. Nearly two-thirds of Americans, according to various surveys, no longer found the war in Afghanistan worth fighting. Not only did Obama fail to take complete ownership of the war that he had once described as the necessary one but he also failed to bridge the differences among his advisers even as a perception started gaining ground that the war was going nowhere for the NATO forces.

Looking for an exit, Obama took the extraordinary

decision in December 2009 of sending 30,000 more US troops to Afghanistan along with the announcement of an American withdrawal from July 2011. This decision led US adversaries to conclude that Obama's heart was not in the war and that he had no will to fight. What was equally confounding was the basis on which Obama made this decision. After repeatedly arguing during elections that Afghanistan was the 'good' war—the 'necessary' war—he started searching for an exit strategy because he couldn't 'lose the whole Democratic Party'[1]. As veteran American journalist Bob Woodward has argued, 'He [Obama] was looking for choices that would limit US involvement and provide a way out.'[2]

The pace of the withdrawal from 2011, however, was not clear, with defence department officials describing the initial reductions as minor and some of Obama's other advisers, including Vice-President Joe Biden, saying the pullout would be as rapid as the deployment of the surge troops. There was confusion all around, and India was also affected by these shifts in American strategy.

INDIA'S AFGHAN OPTIONS

As discussed previously, since 2001, India has primarily relied on its 'soft power' in wooing Kabul. It is one of the largest aid donors to Afghanistan and is delivering humanitarian assistance as well as helping in nation-building projects in myriad ways. India is building roads, providing medical facilities and helping with educational programmes in an effort to develop and enhance long-term local Afghan capabilities. India would be loath to see the political and economic capital it has invested in Afghanistan go to waste. Because India was not consulted prior to the announcement of plans for the withdrawal of American forces by the Obama administration, and because there has been little attempt to make India part of the larger process of ensuring a stable Afghanistan post 2014, a perception has grown in New Delhi that it is on its own if it has to secure its vital interests in Afghanistan.

India has growing stakes in peace and stability in Afghanistan, and the India–Afghan strategic partnership agreement underlines India's commitment to ensuring that a positive momentum in Delhi–Kabul ties is maintained. The Obama administration's reliance on the Pakistani security establishment to help organize and kick-start reconciliation talks aimed at ending the war in Afghanistan, despite accusing the ISI of secretly supporting the Haqqani Network, has been a source of worry for New Delhi. The Pakistani military and the ISI in particular have little interest in bringing the Haqqanis to the negotiating table as they continue to view the insurgents as their best bet for maintaining influence in Afghanistan as the US reduces its presence there.

Therefore, despite the Obama administration's attempt to reach out to India on Afghanistan after its initial blunders, New Delhi has been expecting anarchy to intensify in the region as insurgents in Afghanistan have been repeatedly successful in undermining local and international confidence in the viability of extant political structures in Kabul amidst the withdrawal of Western forces from Afghanistan. Insulating India from the widening disorder will remain the main strategic objective of Delhi's policy towards Afghanistan and Pakistan. New Delhi will have to ensure that it does not lose out as in the past as new realities emerge in the region in the coming years.

It has rightly been observed that India may not be a 'primary' player in Afghanistan but it is an important secondary one with an ability to influence the calculus of the US.[3] While the debate over how to approach Afghanistan is not close to a resolution in Indian political corridors, any change in strategy will have serious implications for the future of India's rise as a global power and regional security in South Asia. And more often than not, India is forgotten in Western media analysis of the situation in Afghanistan, which largely focuses on the West and Pakistan. Should it relinquish its 'soft power' strategy and replace it with something more forceful, that may change.

In recognizing that the borderlands between Pakistan and Afghanistan constitute the single most important threat to global peace and security, arguing that Islamabad is part of the problem rather than the solution, and asking India to join an international concert in managing the Af–Pak region, the US has indeed made significant departures from its traditional posture towards South Asia. India, therefore, will definitely benefit by coordinating its counter-terror strategy with the American one. It has also been suggested that India should try to address Pakistan's fears of Indian meddling on its western frontiers, unfounded as they might be, and should not even hesitate in reaching out to the Pakistani army.[4]

The India–Pakistan divide continues to hang over the future of Afghanistan. Even though there has been a relative ease in bilateral tensions, the two sides continue to have divergent strategic goals in pursuing a peace process. India's premise largely has been that the process will persuade Pakistan to cease supporting and sending extremists into India and start building good neighbourly ties. Pakistan, in contrast, has viewed the process as a means to nudge India to make concessions on Kashmir such as easing of travel restrictions across the Line of Control. Yet it is obvious that India would not give up its control over the Kashmir Valley. And just as India has had difficulty thinking of what it would offer, Pakistan also has had a hard time articulating what it would be satisfied with, short of Kashmir.

The result of all this has been a lack of substantive dialogue between India and Pakistan despite several attempts to initiate discussions. The border situation, in fact, has taken a turn for the worse. The Indo-Pakistan border saw some of the worst violence in 2013 since the 2003 ceasefire, and terrorist infiltration from Pakistan in 2013 was at a five-year high.[5] Though the two countries have tried to keep their border skirmishes from turning into an international crisis, with an impending withdrawal of US forces from Afghanistan, things can deteriorate rapidly. It will be back to business as usual for the Pakistani security establishment and its proxies, with reports already emerging of a large number of Pakistani insurgents sneaking into Indian territory.

Given the current predicament, it is difficult to be optimistic that the peace process will move much beyond initial pleasantries. However, the two sides can aim to maintain the current thaw in their relations. Outsiders, especially the US, can help. Washington should push towards greater internal political and institutional reforms in Pakistan to help the country's leaders better visualize a future of peaceful coexistence with India. The US, meanwhile, should reassure India that it will deal strongly with terrorism emanating from Pakistan, whether directed at Afghanistan or at India. There is a fundamental convergence between American and Indian interests in making sure that a stable, secure Afghanistan, able and willing to live peacefully with its neighbours, emerges in the future. Greater Indian involvement in shaping Afghanistan's future will help Washington in managing the transition to the post-2014 environment much more effectively.

There has been a persistent complaint in the corridors of power in New Delhi that the Obama administration has sacrificed Indian interests at the altar of pleasing Pakistan, which further allowed Pakistan's proxies to destabilize Afghanistan. Now that Washington has made it clear that it views Pakistan as part of the problem and India as part of the solution, New Delhi and Washington have a historic opportunity to work together in bringing stability and security in Afghanistan. Washington's reliance on New Delhi to maintain some semblance of stability in Afghanistan is likely to increase as it will seek to maintain a small, but potent, military presence in Afghanistan at a time of growing recognition of Pakistan's duplicitous behaviour in the corridors of power in the US.

As discussed previously, India's centrality to Afghanistan's future was underscored by the Taliban's statement after then US Secretary of Defence Leon Panetta's visit to India in June 2012. The outfit sought to drive a wedge between New Delhi and Washington by suggesting that India had given a 'negative' answer to Panetta's wish for greater Indian involvement in Afghanistan.[6] This was immediately refuted by the US department of state, which underscored India's important role in regional security, including the transition in Afghanistan.[7] American perception of Indian involvement in Afghanistan has definitely undergone a significant change. India is viewed as a partner in ensuring future stability of Afghanistan. The US is backing a more robust Indian involvement in Afghanistan, signalling a long-term commitment to Afghanistan's future. As part of the third US–India strategic dialogue in June 2012, India and the US announced regular trilateral consultations with Afghanistan.[8] The first trilateral meeting between Afghanistan, India and the US was held on the sidelines of the United Nations General Assembly's annual session in October 2012. It focused on Afghanistan's economic future as well as on the development of roads and rail networks to embed Afghanistan in a broader regional framework.[9] This meeting was described as marking 'the beginning of a series of consultations among the three governments ... who have pledged to work together on common challenges and opportunities, including combating terrorism and violent extremism ... increasing regional trade, investment and integration'[10].

There has been a broader maturing of the US–India defence ties, and Afghanistan will clearly be a beneficiary of this trend. Deeper military relations with India are important for the US in order to address a range of strategic interests which are common to both, and these include the security of the sea lanes of communications in the Indian Ocean, countering terrorism and tackling humanitarian and natural disasters. With India holding more military exercises with the US than with any other country, this convergence is already manifest, but the challenge remains in making this defence engagement more operationally robust.

The US has asked India to place liaison officers in the US Pacific and Central Commands, America's Unified Combatant Commands, which bodes well not only for the future of US–India ties but also for the larger regional security priorities of the two states. But the two sides clearly need to think more cogently as to how this US–India convergence on Afghanistan can be harnessed for mutual ends. America's 'hard power' and India's 'soft power' can be a potent force in the transformation of Afghanistan. The fact that India is part of the Pacific Command whereas Pakistan and Afghanistan lie in the Central Command continues to hinder the policy priorities of Washington and New Delhi. This division of responsibilities compartmentalizes South Asia in ways that are not very helpful, and a realignment will be needed if the US withdrawal proceeds as desired by the Obama administration. The US defence bureaucracy will have to be organized in a way that allows Washington to view the India–Pakistan–Afghanistan matrix in a holistic manner if the US's regional security priorities are to be achieved.

The US and India can also work towards placing an Indian army liaison officer in the International Security Assistance Force (ISAF) headquarters at Kabul. The two can consider having Indian military trainers as part of ISAF to train Afghan security forces. There have been some suggestions that some of the US hardware that will become surplus when US withdrawal begins could be offered to India at concessional prices. These could include some of the items that may be especially useful in dealing with cross-border incursions such as thermal imaging, night vision equipment, some artillery items, improvised explosive device (IED) locators and IED-hardened vehicles. Once India is familiar with US equipment, it could also be a base for training Afghan security forces in their use.[11] But, ultimately, how Washington and New Delhi deal with Pakistan will determine the possibility of obtaining a sustainable outcome in Afghanistan.

How Do You Solve a Problem Like Pakistan?

Pakistan remains the key to success in defeating the Taliban and eliminating Al Qaeda's activities in the region, even as the Obama administration has grown increasingly impatient with its ally for dragging its feet on militant sanctuaries in border areas. As Woodward revealed in his book *Obama's Wars*, fears about Pakistan—a nuclear power with a fragile civilian government, a dominant military and an intelligence service that sponsored terrorist groups—have shaped the trajectory of Obama's Af–Pak policy.[12] The US increasingly views Pakistan as a dishonest partner, unwilling or unable to stop elements of its intelligence service from giving clandestine aid, weapons and money to the Afghan Taliban. Obama himself made it clear to Woodward that 'the cancer is in Pakistan'[13]. For Obama, the reason to create a secure, self-governing Afghanistan was to prevent the spread of the 'cancer' from Pakistan. Pakistan's main priority has been to take on the TTP, its home-grown branch of the Taliban. But the links between the TTP and other terrorist organizations are much too evident to ignore. The US has also pressured Pakistan on the LeT. However, though the Pakistani government is holding Zakiur Rehman Lakhvi, the commander of the Mumbai terror attacks, he 'continues to direct LeT operations from his detention centre'[14], and the LeT has even threatened to carry out attacks in the US.

The priorities of the Pakistani military are also clear. Its retired chief, General Kayani, admitted to the US that his focus remained on India. In Woodward's account, he proudly informed the then US National Security Adviser James Jones, 'I'm India-centric.'[15] Moreover, Pakistan's weak democracy and powerful military and intelligence apparatus has failed to get a grip on terrorism, a problem that now threatens to overwhelm the Pakistani state itself. The Pakistani army's inflexible, India-centric security strategy makes rapprochement with India a nonstarter. Kayani made it clear that he wanted to call the shots in Kabul as he remained wedded to the notion of 'strategic depth'—that is, to making Afghanistan the kind of proprietary hinterland for Pakistan, free of Indian and other outside influence, that it was during 1992–2001.

Given the political dysfunction in Pakistan, which remains deeply divided between an ineffective civilian political elite and a geopolitically overambitious military establishment, Washington and New Delhi will have to work together to contain Pakistan's regional ambitions. Pakistan's domestic institutional fabric remains frayed with tensions not only between the army and the government but the former army chief even warning the judiciary against taking on corrupt military officials. With a limited presence on the Afghan side of the Durand Line and drone strikes on Pakistani soil, Washington intends to keep the pressure on Islamabad to prevent it from unleashing its military–jihadi complex on its regional adversaries once the US starts withdrawing in 2014. Much like New Delhi, Washington views the Pakistani military's continuing support for violent extremism as the greatest obstacle to stability in Afghanistan and to larger regional security.

Despite the reopening of the supply route for NATO by Pakistan in exchange of an apology from then US Secretary of State Hillary Clinton for the killing of Pakistani soldiers in a NATO airstrike in 2012, the relationship between Washington and Islamabad has continued to be tense and the trust deficit remains high. After hitting rock bottom in 2011 after the raid that killed bin Laden and a NATO air strike that killed twenty-four Pakistani soldiers near the country's border with Afghanistan, US–Pakistan relations have become relatively stable with the coming to office of Nawaz Sharif in May 2013. Though the Obama administration decided to release more than $1.5 billion in aid to Pakistan to set a new tone for the bilateral relationship with Pakistan under Sharif, serious differences continue to persist, with Washington pushing Pakistan to take a more robust military posture against the Haqqani Network and other Afghan Taliban groups and Sharif more interested in peace talks with the Pakistani Taliban. That the Pakistani Taliban have little interest in serious talks was evident when they issued a 'to-do' list for Islamabad before they could even think of a ceasefire. The list included clauses like stopping drone attacks, introduction of the sharia law in courts, introduction of the Islamic system of education in public and private institutions, releasing Pakistani and foreign Taliban prisoners, handing over control of tribal areas to local forces, and ending all ties with the US.[16] Pakistan, under Sharif, has also been busy orchestrating the process of political reconciliation by selectively releasing some Taliban leaders, helping with the opening of their office in Qatar and trying to manage their contacts with the US. The Taliban in Pakistan responded to Sharif's peace overtures by stepping up attacks within Pakistan to an extent where Sharif had no choice but to go in for some form of limited military action.

There is widespread concern in Kabul that Pakistan will try to take advantage of the transition phase in Afghanistan to weaken the Afghan government and assert its own influence. As Ismael Qasimyar, Karzai's aide, bluntly put it: Pakistan 'does not want a strong Afghan government; it wants a slice of the cake of Afghan power ... Pakistani officials repeatedly say they want peace and stability for Afghanistan, but Pakistan is a nursery and exporter of extremism. Taliban leaders living in Pakistan need to get out of there, so they will be free to think and be independent and engage in peace.'[17] The American refusal to militarily confront Pakistan, where much of the Taliban leadership resides, is a source of near-universal frustration in Afghanistan as the Taliban are widely considered a proxy force for Pakistan. Pakistan's role in the 'peace process' with the Taliban is viewed with suspicion in Kabul as Islamabad pushed for a power sharing arrangement in which the Taliban would control the eastern and southern provinces in Afghanistan. This is, quite understandably, anathema to the Afghan elites who view this as Pakistan's strategy of undermining the Afghan state. Pakistan's future itself is becoming less certain. As Pakistani journalist Khaled Ahmed aptly notes: 'Pakistan has sought to appease terrorism by becoming anti-American and pro-Taliban. After the withdrawal [of Western forces], a Talibanized Afghanistan will only survive if Pakistan takes its policy of appeasement to its logical end and becomes a caliphate itself.'[18]

Managing Pakistan will be the biggest priority for both Washington and New Delhi in the coming years if there is any hope of keeping Afghanistan a stable entity post 2014. As US–India defence engagement gains momentum, greater consultation on Pakistan should remain a priority. And if Islamabad agrees, the US can think of initiating a US–India–Pakistan dialogue on Afghanistan. Otherwise, transition to a post-2014 Afghanistan will be a difficult one and will pose serious challenges to all three.

A DIFFICULT TRANSITION

In May 2012, during Barack Obama's surprise visit to Kabul to mark bin Laden's death a year back, Washington and Kabul signed the much-awaited Strategic Partnership Agreement (SPA), which stipulates that the Afghan security forces would take the lead in combat operations by the end of the following year and most American troops would leave by the end of 2014.[19] The pact underscored America's commitment to Afghanistan for a decade after its formal troop withdrawal in 2014 as this withdrawal would not include trainers who would continue to assist Afghan forces and a contingent of troops tasked with combating Al Qaeda through counterterrorism operations. Washington hoped that this pact would provide some much-needed clarity about America's intended footprint in Afghanistan over the next decade, though specific details were yet to be finalized. For Washington, the imperative was to extract itself from the war in Afghanistan and focus its attention on more significant geopolitical challenges emanating from the rise of China. The Taliban responded to the pact by asserting that the strategic partnership between Kabul and Washington 'gave legitimacy to the occupation of Afghanistan and will lead to further insecurity and political instability'[20].

Afghanistan's national security advisor Rangin Dadfar Spanta described the pact as 'providing a strong foundation for the security of Afghanistan, the region and the world, and is a document for the development of the region'. He was of course right in so far as this pact removed the uncertainty and ambiguity surrounding America's post-2014 posture in Afghanistan, especially for New Delhi, which had been concerned about the serious implications for Indian security of American withdrawal. The US made it clear that it sought 'an enduring partnership with Afghanistan that strengthens Afghan sovereignty, stability and prosperity and that contributes to our shared goal of defeating Al Qaeda and its extremist affiliates'. It was towards that end that the pact underscored the ongoing American role in bolstering Afghan democracy and civil society and pledged American financial support to Afghanistan till 2024. Washington wanted to send a signal that it would not abandon Afghanistan and would retain a presence in the evolving strategic realities in the region.

This was also a signal to the Taliban and other extremist groups that waiting out American forces might no longer be as credible an option as it would have seemed before. Washington's message had particular resonance in India and Pakistan. Pakistan came under renewed pressure to articulate a long-term policy of renouncing its ties with the extremist groups. The hedging strategy that the country's army had been relying on came under stress, with Pakistan's dilemma about the collusion between the Afghan and Pakistan Taliban and the growing challenge of the Taliban to Pakistan getting accentuated with each passing day. Pakistan recognized the difficulty of managing a post-America neighbourhood, with Pashtuns inside Pakistan and Afghanistan asserting their profile. Moreover, the larger reality was that Pakistan was weaker than at any other time in its history. With its economy in a shambles, the sectarian divide growing, and the extremist groups it had nurtured turning against the state, it had no real friends left, with even China preferring to maintain a respectful distance.

Notwithstanding the SPA, the final passage of the Bilateral Security Agreement (BSA) that defines terms and conditions for the residual military presence in Afghanistan post 2014, and as part of which the US could keep up to 15,000 troops in Afghanistan after 2014 for the purposes of counterterrorism and training of Afghan forces, was a difficult one. This on-again, off-again security pact between the US and Afghanistan became mired in differences between

Washington and Karzai, with both indulging in brinkmanship. Karzai, with his actions, made it clear that he was not too eager to have a residual US presence in Afghanistan and tended to postpone a final agreement with the US. The US, meanwhile, reached out to other stakeholders such as Afghan Defence Minister Bismillah Khan Mohammadi, army chief General Sher Mohammad Karimi and Deputy Interior Minister Mohammad Ayub Salangi. Karzai underscored that he would sign the long-term security pact with the US only if the US helped his government begin peace talks with the Taliban and agreed to release all seventeen Afghan citizens being held in Guantanamo Bay, its military prison in Cuba. The US retaliated by making it clear that if the agreement was not signed, US forces would begin planning for a complete withdrawal at the end of 2014. The NATO countries also underlined that they would not be able to leave even small forces behind in Afghanistan without guarantees from Karzai.

Amidst political uncertainty in Afghanistan and war weariness in the US, Obama announced in May 2014 that the US would leave a residual force of 9,800 troops in Afghanistan after the NATO-led combat mission in the country ended in 2014 and that nearly all troops would be gone by the end of 2016, dropping to just the security contingent for the US embassy in Kabul. The BSA, as drafted by the US, had outlined an American military mission that could remain active 'until the end of 2024 and beyond'. This was interpreted in Afghanistan and beyond that the US would maintain a troop presence in the country until at least 2024. Obama's abrupt announcement increased anxiety in the region, with Afghans themselves caught off-guard by the speed with which the American forces would be withdrawn.[21]

US Defence Secretary Chuck Hagel admitted that there remained a lot of unanswered questions about how many of the nearly 10,000 US personnel remaining in Afghanistan after 2014 would be devoted to the counterterrorism mission. It was also not clear how many NATO and other international partners of the US would contribute and what exactly those forces would do. US officials acknowledged that there was 'a certain amount of anxiety across the region about what the transition in Afghanistan means', but Washington did little to assuage these anxieties. Instead, it made foreign policy choices based primarily on the domestic political calculus.[22]

Obama announced that the US would withdraw all of its military forces from Afghanistan by the end of 2016, irrespective of the facts on the ground. And the Obama administration's decision to swap five of the hardest cases at Guantanamo for the release of Sergeant Bowe Bergdahl from the Taliban in May 2014 also sent a message of retreat.[23] Bergdahl was a captive of the Taliban-aligned Haqqani Network in Afghanistan from June 2009. The success of the Taliban's hostage-taking in conjunction with Obama's withdrawal pledge only convinced the Taliban that they could keep fighting while the two sides talked and still win. Not surprising then that Taliban chief Mullah Omar described the group's negotiated release of the prisoners as a 'great victory'. Though both Washington and the Taliban rejected the suggestion that the prisoner exchange might lead to a rejuvenation of the effort to engage the Taliban in a peace process, the deal ended up conferring the kind of legitimacy on the Taliban leadership that the US had sought to avoid.[24]

New Delhi, for its part, was at a loss to respond to the rapidly changing ground realities in its immediate neighbourhood. Despite complaints from India about shifting messages from Washington, New Delhi needed to put its own house in order—which never happened. As Washington and Kabul were coming to terms with each other for a post-2014 milieu, New Delhi should have taken the opportunity to assert its role as a more credible actor in its neighbourhood. The Washington–Kabul Strategic Partnership Agreement provided India with crucial space for diplomatic manoeuvring so as to regain the lost ground and expand its footprint in a neighbouring state where it remained hugely popular despite a certain ambivalence regarding its potential to deliver.

An attempt to beef up intelligence sharing between India and Afghanistan in 2012 was the first step in the operationalization of the Indo-Afghan strategic partnership but more such concrete steps are needed to ensure that New Delhi maintains a substantial presence in Afghanistan. India can offer training to Afghan security forces in counter-insurgency, given its long experience in dealing with multiple insurgencies within its own borders. Afghanistan has asked India to step up its role in the training of Afghan security forces, including the police, and this offer should be seized by New Delhi. Indian defence officials have made a strong case for sending training teams to Afghanistan to train Afghan personnel and assist the country in establishing its own training institutions. Kabul needs substantive military cooperation from New Delhi if it is to take on the offensive of its adversaries effectively.[25]

And yet in May 2013, when Karzai gave a 'wish list' of defence supplies to India that included 105-mm howitzer artillery, medium-lift aircraft, bridge-laying equipment and trucks, it was too much for India. This demand reflected a growing concern in Kabul that Afghan soldiers were woefully unprepared for the kind of fighting that might result with the Taliban militants after the departure of Western forces in 2014. Kabul was keen to diversify its defence relationships and sought an expansive defence partnership with India. But New Delhi rejected Karzai's demand in the hope that such a gesture might help Sharif regain some leverage vis-à-vis the military in reinventing Pakistan's India policy.

This Afghan demand was repeated in December 2013 and again in June 2014 after the coming to power of the Modi government in Delhi. By not taking these requests seriously, New Delhi lost traction in Kabul without gaining any goodwill in Pakistan even as it further marginalized itself in the unfolding drama in its neighbourhood. Though New Delhi ended up finalizing a pact with Moscow to supply arms to Afghanistan, under which India would pay for the military equipment that would be sourced from Russia, the exact ramifications of this decision remained a matter of speculation.[26] India also remained opposed to setting up any military training facility in Afghanistan as demanded by Kabul.

On the economic front too, the Indian corporate sector needs reassurances from the Indian government that its efforts in Afghanistan would not go waste and that the might of the Indian state is with it. The Indian private sector has been unwilling to expand its footprint in Afghanistan in any significant manner because of security concerns. Where the state-funded Chinese companies can count on state support, there has been no such help from the Indian government to the nation's corporate sector. At the same time, India has not been successful in building linkages with the Taliban's Quetta Shura though there have been numerous opportunities. The consequences of this lackadaisical Indian approach are likely to be rather serious.

The risks to South Asian security from a failure in Afghanistan are great. As US troops draw down from 9,800 in early 2015, it is likely that the counterterrorism effort will end long before the overall mission concludes, lacking sufficient troop strength to conduct those operations. This could lead to a resurgence of hardened militants, encouraging the Taliban to fight on, motivating Pakistan to maintain its support for the insurgents as a hedge and sowing insecurity among Afghans.[27] Abandoning the goal of establishing a functioning Afghan state and a moderate Pakistan would place greater pressure on Indian security. Pakistani intelligence would be emboldened to escalate terrorist attacks against India once it is satisfied that the Taliban would provide it strategic depth in Afghanistan. This would surely force retaliation from India. Indian defence officials have been warning the Indian military brass to be on guard to tackle any spillover effect in Jammu and Kashmir and elsewhere due to Pakistan's continuing support to the Taliban and its inroads into Afghanistan.[28]

Indian intelligence services have termed the withdrawal

of Western forces from Afghanistan as one of the biggest challenges to India's counterterrorism measures as, in their estimation, this is likely to lead to a substantive increase in terrorism and infiltration attempts along the border with Pakistan.[29] Moreover, there are already signs that the Al Qaeda is attempting a comeback in Afghanistan's mountainous eastern sector as the Western forces prepare to draw down. The Al Qaeda has been building ties with like-minded Islamic militant groups, including the LeT, and its ties with the Haqqani Network remain strong.[30] LeT founder Hafiz Saeed is eagerly waiting for US withdrawal from Afghanistan to revive militancy in Kashmir.[31] Saeed's LeT not only continues to launch terror attacks in India but is now increasingly targeting Indian interests in Afghanistan with help from the Haqqani Network.

India is the new target, with one Al Qaeda cleric, Asim Umar, calling on Indian Muslims to battle for sharia rule, and another, Ahmad Farooq, claiming 'to hasten our advance towards Delhi'[32]. In June 2014, a video was released by the Al Qaeda, urging Kashmiri youths to use violence against the Indian presence in Kashmir as opposed to democratic protest.[33] Against the backdrop of an imploding West Asia, it is highly unlikely that South Asia would be able to remain immune from the victory of extremist forces in Iraq and Syria.

As a consequence, a peace deal in Afghanistan that gives Pakistan and its Taliban friends a dominating role in Afghanistan is an unwelcome development for New Delhi. Rewarding bad behaviour would only embolden more hostility, a reasonable conclusion because of its past experience, making New Delhi even more reluctant to pursue a 'peace process' with Islamabad. A replay of the tragic circumstances Afghanistan encountered between 1994 and 2001 will not only plunge the country into a Hobbesian civil war but will have deleterious effects for regional security. India would be one of the biggest casualties, and a large part of the blame for this would have to be shouldered by New Delhi.

INDIA ON THE DEFENSIVE

Every few years, foreign policy establishments in Washington and London get down to brass tacks and try to find answers to the perennial instability in South Asia. And, every time, the bright minds ignore the evidence staring them in their faces and conclude that it is India that is a large part of the problem. It is happening again as the West prepares to leave Afghanistan and wants a convenient alibi as to why the situation in Afghanistan is so difficult to resolve. The West is once again ready to buy—lock, stock and barrel—into the Pakistani line that sorting out Kashmir is the way to final peace in Afghanistan.

The Obama administration is under pressure to make pragmatic compromises with the Taliban. The US has been in touch with the Taliban for years now. After some back-channel attempts, Washington remains desperate for some sort of a modus vivendi with the Taliban. Despite Karzai's reservations, his government has no credible military apparatus to make it a serious player in the game.

The 2009 surge of an additional 30,000 troops was a half-hearted measure by Washington, and the results are evident on the ground, with southern provinces facing the rising tide of insurgency and the formerly secure north and west of the country back into being contested areas. With the deadline of 2014 looming ever closer, the US abandoned its demands that Pakistan crack down on Taliban safe havens as it needed Pakistan's help to bring the Taliban to the negotiating table.

Pakistan's security establishment is in chest-thumping mood for being recognized as the central player in the Afghanistan dynamic. Its critical role in bringing the Taliban to the negotiating table is well appreciated in Washington and London. It doesn't really matter that, for all these years, the Pakistani military had been vehemently denying that it had any leverage over the Taliban.

Forced by India, Washington has underlined that 'any political settlement must result in the Taliban breaking ties with the Al Qaeda, renouncing violence, and accepting the Afghan constitution, including its protection for all Afghans, women and men'. The reality, however, is that the peace process is a sham, and, merely to get the Taliban on board, Washington agreed to let Mullah Omar come to the negotiating table without acceding to any of the 'red lines'. There has been no acceptance of the Afghan constitution as was reflected in the title of the office that the Taliban opened in Doha—the Islamic Emirate of Afghanistan. The Taliban have refused to recognize the Afghan government and to cut ties with the Al Qaeda. There has been no ceasefire on the ground or even an attempt to delink Afghanistan from global terrorism. Moreover, even the Haqqani Network has been given a seat at the table at the Pakistani army's behest.

The Taliban are well aware of how eager Washington and London are to end the war in Afghanistan at any cost, and they are willing to play to their weakness. A myth is being sold in Washington and London as high strategy that the Taliban are interested in sharing power. There is no empirical or historical basis to support this claim.

Yet it is being made repeatedly and is now almost conventional wisdom in Washington and London's power circle. There is going to be no reconciliation out of this peace process, only a face-saving interregnum for a smooth disengagement of the ISAF from Afghanistan. It must be remembered that the Clinton administration also tried to negotiate with the Taliban with disastrous results for the US and the world.

The US has failed to reassure New Delhi that Washington will not compromise on its demands that the Taliban break its ties with international terrorist networks and participate in a normal political process. New Delhi has made itself marginal in Afghanistan, and it has no one but itself to blame. Recognizing the inevitable, India too has signalled that it is willing to engage with the 'good Taliban'—those groups that are willing to join the mainstream. With the prevailing wisdom in the West making India the culprit in Afghanistan, what is not clear is if anyone is interested in talking to India. While the West ponders the prospects of bringing peace to Afghanistan, it needs to recognize the real source of problems in the region. Buying the loyalty of the Taliban or accepting a Pakistani-brokered deal in Kabul will only pave the way for another, perhaps even more dangerous, conflict involving terrorist groups and nuclear armed neighbours. By pursuing a strategy that might end up giving Pakistan the leading role in the state structures in Afghanistan, the West might just be sowing the seeds for future regional turmoil. In its desperation to get out of Afghanistan, the Obama administration might be taking an approach that will do more harm than good over the long term.

Facing the collapse of the nation-building project in Afghanistan on the one hand and Pakistan's rising influence on the other, India's policy in Afghanistan stands at a crossroads. The world's eyes are on India to do some heavy lifting in Afghanistan after 2014. Where a militarized, economically bust Pakistan has little to offer to Afghanistan's future, a democratic India with a growing economy should emerge as natural partner for Afghanistan. Though the US presence in Afghanistan since 2001 has been beneficial for India, ultimately India will have to fight its own battles as the US starts moving out of Afghanistan. As a consequence, the Indian footprint in Afghanistan should increase if it wants to preserve its vital interests. The Pakistani military has become adept at the double game it has been playing with Washington. It recognizes America's continuing reliance on Pakistan, and it will extract its pound of flesh from the West.

As the threat of instability increases, the centrality of the Pakistani military is only likely to grow. And given the anti-India mindset that sustains the Pakistani military's privileged position in the Pakistani society, New Delhi would be fooling itself if it believes that negotiations with Islamabad and Rawalpindi are likely to lead to any sort of a desirable outcome. The Taliban seem to think that they are winning in

Afghanistan and so have little incentive to come to any sort of accommodation with the Karzai government or the West. The Pakistani security establishment continues to believe that the Taliban will eventually come back to power in Kabul and so it has no desire to disavow its age-old connections with the Taliban.

Given the high stakes involved, India has no option but to take a leading role in foreign policy in its neighbourhood, especially when it comes to Af–Pak. It is no one's case that New Delhi should ignore the regional consequences of a more assertive Afghan policy, but it cannot ignore the dangers that will flow from the Pakistani military's likely advances in Afghanistan after 2014. India should not shy away from a proactive engagement with the civilian leadership in Pakistan, but it cannot be an excuse for not extending strong military support for Kabul.

Instead of ignoring Delhi, the West would also be better served if it ceases to pander to Pakistan for short-term gains. Not supporting the only secular liberal democracy in the region will only embolden the radical Islamists in the long term. And that's no way to enhance regional security. There is a real danger that the withdrawal of American troops would be seen by regional powers as an invitation for a revival of the nineteenth century's 'Great Game'. The withdrawal will be portrayed by Washington as a substantive achievement of the Obama administration, even though the ability of the Afghan government to withstand the onslaught of the Taliban remains far from clear. It might end up being a repeat of the fateful US mistake of abandoning the country after the Soviet withdrawal in 1989, which opened the way to a civil war that brought the Taliban to power and created a haven for the Al Qaeda.

For India, Afghanistan should be a strategic priority. It enjoys immense goodwill among ordinary Afghans that it has earned by its decade-long investment in Afghanistan. Manmohan Singh's visit to Kabul in May 2011 was a signal to the world that India remained a major player in the evolving ground realities in the region even as the West tried to find a modus vivendi with the Taliban. But since then, the UPA-II government, distracted by perennial turmoil in the domestic political scene, ignored Afghanistan, causing much damage to Indian interests and credibility. The next government would need to revitalize India's approach towards Afghanistan with a new sense of purpose.

The political leadership in New Delhi cannot ignore the turmoil in the neighbourhood. Urgent ameliorative measures are needed if India is to regain the initiative in Afghanistan. Blaming Pakistan or the US will no longer serve any purpose if Indian interests get jeopardized like in the past because of New Delhi's own callousness. And while making the most of US–India convergence, Indian policy cannot rely solely on American benevolence. It will have to work on a number of fronts: convince the West that, despite its military departure, it should continue its diplomatic and economic engagement with Afghanistan; continue to work towards strengthening Afghan political, bureaucratic and civil society institutional fabric; reach out to Russia, Iran and other Central Asian states and make an effort to convince China to put greater pressure on Pakistan to mend its ways; ramp up its intelligence activities in Pakistan and Afghanistan; and, finally, get ready to support the Afghan government militarily.

It cannot be one or the other, nor should there be an expectation that Indian interests would be taken care of by others. This means, in the ultimate analysis, instilling a sense of urgency that should be associated with any endeavour like this one to protect vital national interests, in which India has been so clearly losing ground. Acting decisively in Afghanistan will have some costs for sure, but indecisiveness has been exacting its own cost, which will only rise if India decides to take a back seat. India still has a small window of opportunity to emerge as a credible alternative in Afghanistan. If it fails to make use of this window, it will be forced to fight a rearguard action, and the only option available might be to support elements of the Northern Alliance as in the past in the context of civil war in Afghanistan.

India has refused to fight in the Afghan war because of the pretence that it is America's war. Now the war is likely to come to India's shores, and Delhi will have to respond not only to preserve its equities in Afghanistan but also to protect it from the negative externalities of the changing regional geopolitics. And that would mean taking some risks and, in particular, taking the war to Afghanistan, choosing the time and place on India's own terms as opposed to fighting a war on terms defined by its adversaries.

Alexis de Tocqueville, the French political thinker, once said: 'When the past no longer illuminates the future, the spirit walks in darkness.' India will certainly be surrounded by darkness if the nation's policymakers do not learn from the past and shape a different future for Afghanistan, India and the region.

NOTES

Preface

1. Vijaita Singh, 'IB told Rajnath: NATO troops withdrawal from Afghan will up infiltration, terror activities,' *Indian Express*, 16 June 2014.
2. Lalit K. Jha, 'LeT behind attack on Indian consulate in Herat, says US,' *Indian Express*, 27 June 2014.

Introduction

1. Shubhajit Roy, 'Want defence ties boost with India, says Afghan envoy,' *Indian Express*, 17 May 2013.
2. Rani D. Mullen, 'The India–Afghanistan Partnership,' India Development Cooperation Research Bilateral Brief, 16 May 2013.
3. Jawaharlal Nehru, *India's Foreign Policy: Selected Speeches, September 1946-April 1961* (Delhi: Government of India, 1961), 113–114.
4. For a detailed explication of Indian thinking about New Delhi's approach towards its immediate neighbourhood and its link to India's larger foreign policy priorities, see A. Martin Wainwright, 'Regional Security and Paramount Powers: The British Raj and Independent India', in Chetan Kumar

and Marvin G. Weinbaum, eds., *South Asia Approaches the Millennium: Reexamining National Security* (Oxford: Westview Press, 1995), 41–62.

5. Ahmad Nadem and Ahmad Haroon, 'Sixteen Afghan civilians killed in rogue US attack,' Reuters, 11 March 2012.

6. Matthew Rosenberg and Rod Nordland, 'US Abandoning Hopes for Taliban Peace Deal,' *New York Times*, 1 October 2012.

7. Peter Baker, 'Rebutting Critics, Obama Seeks Higher Bar for Military Action,' *International New York Times*, 28 May 2014.

8. Eli Lake, 'As Obama Draws Down, Al Qaeda Grows in Afghanistan,' *Daily Beast*, 29 May 2014.

9. Elisabeth Bumiller and Allison Kopicki, 'Support for Afghan War Falls in US, Poll Finds,' *New York Times*, 26 March 2012; Rob Winnett and Peter Foster, 'Britain wants endgame in Afghanistan, says David Cameron,' *Daily Telegraph*, 14 March 2012.

10. Ian Traynor, 'Nato withdrawal from Afghanistan could be speeded up, says Rasmussen,' *Guardian*, 1 October 2012.

11. Elisabeth Bumiller and Allison Kopicki, 'Support for Afghan War Falls in US, Poll Finds,' *New York Times*, 26 March 2012; Rob Winnett and Peter Foster, 'Britain wants endgame in Afghanistan, says David Cameron,' *Daily Telegraph*, 14 March 2012.

12. Elisabeth Bumiller, 'US to End Combat Role in Afghanistan as Early as Next Year, Panetta Says,' *New York Times*, 1 February 2012.

13. Mark Landler, 'Obama Signs Pact in Kabul, Turning Page in Afghan War,' *New York Times*, 1 May 2012.

14. Anne Gearan, 'US, Afghanistan reach agreement on outline of post-2014 security deal,' *Washington Post*, 12 October 2013.

15. Daniel Markey, 'The Nixon Test,' *Indian Express*, 24 October 2012.

16. Rajiv Chandrasekaran, 'Afghan security forces' rapid expansion comes at a cost as readiness lags,' *Washington Post*, 22 October 2012.

17. Frud Bezhan, 'Former Afghan Warlord Remobilizes Militia,' *Radio Free Europe*, 14 November 2012, http://www.rferl. org/content/afghanistan-former-mujahedin-warlord-recalls-militia/24771179.html

18. 'India, US tightlipped on waiver from Iran oil sanctions,' *Rediff*, 8 June 2012, available at http://www.rediff.com/ news/report/india-us-tightlipped-on-waiver-from-iran-oil-sanctions/20120608.htm

INDIAN INTERESTS IN AFGHANISTAN

1. This very brief historical overview is by no means a definitive historical account. It is derived from a number of sources including Louis Dupree, *Afghanistan* (Princeton, New Jersey: Princeton University Press, 1980); Larry P. Goodson, *Afghanistan's Endless War: State Failure, Regional Politics and the Rise of the Taliban* (Washington: University of Washington Press, 2001); J.C. Griffiths, *Afghanistan* (London: Pall Mall Press, 1967); Angelo Rasanayagam, *Afghanistan: A Modern History* (London, New York: I.B. Tauris & Co., 2003); and Stephen Tanner, *Afghanistan: A Military History from Alexander the Great to the Fall of the Taliban* (Cambridge, MA: Da Capo Press, 2003).

2. Martin Ewans, *Afghanistan: A New History* (Great Britain: Curzon Press, 2002), 1.

3. Milan Hauner, *The Soviet War in Afghanistan* (USA: University Press of America, 1991), 101.

4. Ibid., 88.

5. Geraint Hughes, 'The Soviet–Afghan War, 1978–1989: An Overview,' *Defence Studies*, Vol. 8, No. 3 (2008): 326-350.

6. Seth Jones, *In the Graveyard of Empires* (USA: W.W. Norton & Company Inc., 2009), 25.

7. Marvin G. Weinbaum, 'Pakistan and Afghanistan: The Strategic Relationship,' *Asian Survey*, Vol. 31, No. 6 (1991), 498–99.

8. Rifaat Hussain, 'Pakistan's Relations With Afghanistan: Continuity and Change,' *Strategic Studies*, 22(4), 2002, available at http://www.issi.org.pk/journal/2002_files/no_4/article/3a.htm

9. Husain Haqqani, *Pakistan: Between Mosque and Military* (Washington, DC: Carnegie Endowment for International Peace, 2005), 238–260.

10. Pervez Hoodboy, 'The Saudi-isation of Pakistan,' *Newsline*, 1 January 2009.

11. Carlotta Gall, 'Karzai Threatens to Send Soldiers into Pakistan,' *International Herald Tribune*, 16 June 2008.

12. Candace Rondeaux, 'Foreign Agents Blamed in Deadly Kabul Attack,' *Washington Post*, 9 July 2008.

13. C. Raja Mohan, 'India's New Road to Afghanistan,' *Hindu*, 6 September 2003.

14. Rahul Bedi, 'Strategic Realignments,' *Frontline*, 17 April 2003.

15. Seth Jones, 'Pakistan's Dangerous Game,' *Survival*, 49(1), 2007, 15–32.

16. John Negroponte, 'Annual Threat Assessment of the Director of National Intelligence. Testimony to the Senate Select Committee on Intelligence,' 11 January 2007, available at http://intelligence.senate.gov/070111/negroponte.pdf

17. Jane Perlez and Pir Zubair Shah, 'Taliban Losses are No Sure Gain for Pakistanis,' *New York Times*, 28 June 2009.

18. C. Raja Mohan, 'Trade-off on Transit,' *Hindu*, 12 August 2004.

19. Bernard Haykel, 'Radical Salafism,' *Hindu*, 1 December 2001.

20. Charles Allen, *God's Terrorists: The Wahabbi Cult and the Hidden Roots of Modern Jihad* (London: Little, Brown, 2006).

21. A. Rashid, *Taliban: The Story of Afghan Warlords* (Oxford: Pan Books, 2001), 183–187.

22. Rasyul Bakhsh Rais, 'Afghanistan and the Regional Powers,' *Asian Survey*, 33(9), 1993, 915–16.

23. M. Baabar, 'The Call of the Camps,' *Outlook*, 28 August 2006.

24. Mary Anne Weaver, *Pakistan: In the Shadow of Jihad and*

Afghanistan (New York: Farrar, Strauss and Giroux, 2002), 249–272.

25. Husain Haqqani, *Pakistan: Between Mosque and Military* (Washington, DC: Carnegie Endowment for International Peace, 2005), 301–309.

26. N. Subramanian, 'Such a Short Journey,' *Hindu*, 7 July 2009.

27. A. Rashid, *Taliban: The Story of Afghan Warlord* (Oxford: Pan Books, 2001), 207–216.

28. Rahul Bedi, 'India and Central Asia,' *Frontline*, 14 September 2002.

29. Sheela Bhatt, 'India, Tajikistan discuss Afghanistan, counter-terrorism,' *India Abroad*, 3 July 2012.

30. Michael R. Gordon, 'US Says Iranian Arms Seized in Afghanistan,' *New York Times*, 18 April 2007.

31. Michael R. Gordon, 'US Says Iranian Arms Seized in Afghanistan,' *New York Times*, 18 April 2007.

32. Harsh V. Pant, *Contemporary Debates in Indian Foreign and Security Policy: India Negotiates Its Rise in the International System* (New York: Palgrave Macmillan, 2008), 113–129.

33. Stephen Blank, 'US Interests in Central Asia and the Challenges to Them,' (Carlisle, PA: Strategic Studies Institute, US Army War College, 2007), 31–32.

34. Juli A. MacDonald, 'Rethinking India's and Pakistan's Regional Intent,' The National Bureau of Asian Research Analysis, 14(4), 2003, 25.

35. Steve Coll, *Ghost Wars: The Secret Story of the CIA, Afghanistan, and Bin Laden, from the Soviet Invasion to September 10, 2001* (New York: The Penguin Books, 2004), 571.

36. B. Raman, 'Terrorism in Afghanistan and Central Asia,' South Asia Analysis Group, Paper No. 1172, 2004, available at http://www.saag.org/papers12/paper1172.html

37. Karen De Young, 'Obama Outlines Afghan Strategy,' *Washington Post*, 28 March 2009.

38. Pranay Sharma, 'The Lesser Evil?' *Outlook*, 6 April 2009.

39. Ashley Tellis, 'Testimony Before the US Senate Committee on Homeland Security and Governmental Affairs,' 28 January 2009, available at http://hsgac.senate.gov/public/_files/012809Tellis.pdf

INDIA AND AFGHANISTAN: AN EVER-SHIFTING LANDSCAPE SINCE 2001

1. V. Gregorian, *The Emergence of Modern Afghanistan* (Stanford, CA: Stanford University Press, 1969), 91–128.
2. Partha S. Ghosh and Rajaram Panda, 'Domestic Support for Mrs Gandhi's Afghanistan Policy: The Soviet Factor in Indian Politics,' *Asian Survey*, 23(3), 1983, 261–63.
3. Details of Pakistan's ties to the Taliban can be found in Ahmed Rashid, *Taliban* (New Haven: Yale University Press, 2001).
4. Steve Coll, *Ghost Wars: The Secret Story of the CIA, Afghanistan, and Bin Laden, from the Soviet Invasion to September 10, 2001* (New York: The Penguin Books, 2004), 463, 513. This has been corroborated by the author's discussions with senior Indian bureaucrats in the Indian Ministry of External Affairs and Ministry of Defence.
5. See the Statement made by the Indian prime minister at the end of the signing of the first-ever Strategic Partnership Agreement with Afghanistan on 4 October 2011. The text is available at http://www.thehindu.com/news/resources/article2513967.ece
6. On the changing priorities of Indian foreign policy in recent years, see Harsh V. Pant, *Contemporary Debates in Indian Foreign and Security Policy: India Negotiates Its Rise in the International System* (New York: Palgrave Macmillan, 2008).
7. Agreement on Provisional Arrangements in Afghanistan Pending the Re-Establishment of Permanent Government Institutions, Bonn Agreement, United Nations, Bonn, Germany, 5 December 2001, available at http://www.unhcr.org/refworld/docid/3f48f4754.html
8. Press Trust of India, 'India-Afghanistan Blossom Amidst

Turmoil,' 27 December 2006.

9. A. Baruah, 'Karzai Keen on Indian Expertise,' *Hindu*, 22 January 2002.

10. TNN, 'US seal on India's key role in rebuilding Afghanistan,' *Times of India*, 20 October 2012.

11. Bijoyeta Das, 'Afghan students flock to India's universities,' Aljazeera.net, 3 June 2013.

12. V.K. Nambiar, 'Statement on the Situation in Afghanistan at the Security Council', 6 April 2004, available at http://www. un.int/india/2004/ind910.pdf

13. 'Afghanistan: The World Factbook,' Central Intelligence Agency, available at https://www.cia.gov/library/publications/ the-world-factbook/geos/af.html

14. Press Trust of India, 'Afghanistan and the popularity of Bollywood are inseparable,' 17 June 2012.

15. Jason Burke, 'WikiLeaks cables: US diplomats suggested Bollywood starts should tour Afghanistan,' *Guardian*, 16 December 2010.

16. 'Karzai invites India Inc. to invest in Afghanistan,' *Deccan Herald*, 10 November 2012.

17. Eltaf Najafizada, 'Indian Group Wins Rights to Mine in Afghanistan's Hajigak,' Bloomberg, 6 December 2011.

18. G. Srinivasan, 'Afghanistan's entry to SAARC will lead to $2-bn gain for sub-continent,' *Hindu Business Line*, 29 March 2007.

19. Sandeep Singh, 'Want to see India join Afghan trade pact with Pakistan: Karzai,' *Indian Express*, 12 November 2012.

20. 'CEOs should replace generals in Afghanistan, says India,' *Indian Express*, 28 June 2012.

21. Ranjan Mathai, Fifth IISS-MEA Foreign Policy Dialogue Keynote Address, 4 October 2012, available at http://www. iiss.org/en/research/south%20asia%20security/south%20 asia%20conferences/sections/2012-c5b8/fifth-iiss-mea-foreign-policy-dialogue-ec3a/ranjan-mathai-address-5b19

22. Sanjeev Miglani, 'India stepping up to the challenge of post-

2014 Afghanistan,' Reuters, 12 November 2012.

23. 'India hints at Pak link to Kabul Embassy attack,' *Indian Express*, 10 October 2009.

24. 'ISI behind attack on Indian embassy: Afghan envoy to US,' *Indian Express*, 10 October 2009.

25. Matthieu Aikins, 'Following the Money,' *Caravan*, 1 September 2011, available at http://www.caravanmagazine.in/Story/1051/Following-the-Money.html

26. Ashis Ray, 'World Rejects India's Taliban Stand,' *Times of India*, 29 January 2010.

27. Anita Joshua, 'Bid to Placate Pakistan on Afghanistan,' *Hindu*, 4 August 2011.

28. B. Muralidhar Reddy, 'Don't leave Afghanistan, India told US,' *Hindu*, 24 May 2011.

29. 'US Seeks to Balance India's Afghanistan Stake,' Reuters, 1 June 2010.

30. David E. Sanger and Peter Baker, 'Afghanistan Drawdown to Begin in 2011, Officials Say,' *New York Times*, 1 December 2009.

31. 'Fundamentalist regime in Kabul to affect India most,' *Indian Express*, 13 September 2010.

32. Karin Brulliard and Karen De Young, 'Some Afghan military officers to get training in Pakistan,' *Washington Post*, 1 July 2010.

33. Ibid.

34. Miles Amoore, 'Pakistan puppet masters guide the Taliban killers,' *Sunday Times*, 13 June 2010.

35. Greg Jaffe and Karen De Young, 'Leaked files lay bare war in Afghanistan,' *Washington Post*, 26 July 2010.

36. Mark Mazzetti, Jane Perlez, Eric Schmitt and Andrew W. Lehren, 'Pakistan Aids Insurgency in Afghanistan, Reports Assert,' *New York Times*, 25 July 2010.

37. Manu Pubby, 'Evidence of Pak blackmail, how ISI paid Taliban to hit Indians in Kabul,' *Indian Express*, 27 July 2010.

38. Pranab Dhal Samanta, 'The die is cast,' *Indian Express*, 14

May 2011.

39. Jay Solomon and Alan Cullison, 'Islamabad, Kabul Sign Pact,' *Wall Street Journal*, 18 July 2010.

BACK IN THE GAME: TOO LITTLE, TOO LATE?

1. Based on the author's private interview with a senior Indian foreign policy official. For details on the changing trajectory of Indian policy in Afghanistan, see Harsh V. Pant, 'India's Changing Role in Afghanistan,' *Middle East Quarterly*, Vol. 18, No. 2 (Spring 2011), 31–39.

2. Strategic ties with Kabul...India not like US, says PM,' *Indian Express*, 13 May 2011.

3. Teresita and Howard Schaffer, 'India and the US moving closer on Afghanistan?' *Hindu*, 1 June 2011.

4. 'India committed to building the capabilities of Afghan security forces,' *Hindu*, 2 June 2011.

5. Tom Wright and Margherita Stancita, 'Karzai Sets Closer Ties With India on Visit,' *Wall Street Journal*, 5 October 2011.

6. 'CEOs should replace generals in Afghanistan, says India,' *Indian Express*, 28 June 2012.

7. Joshua Partlow, 'Karzai accuses Pakistan of supporting terrorists,' *Washington Post*, 3 October 2011.

8. Julian E. Barnes, Matthew Rosenberg and Adam Entous, 'US Accuses Pakistan of Militant Ties,' *Wall Street Journal*, 23 September 2011.

9. Rajat Pandit, 'US exit: India steps up Afghan army training,' *Times of India*, 13 July 2013.

10. Vladimir Radyuhin, 'India, Russia to step up cooperation in Afghanistan,' *Hindu*, 3 August 2010.

11. Ibid.

12. See 'Putin, in India, Asks Pakistanis to end Support for the Militants,' *New York Times*, 5 December 2002. Also see 'Russia Backs India on Pak,' *Times of India*, 5 December 2002; 'Delhi Declaration Asks Pak to End Infiltration,' *Hindu*,

5 December 2002.

13. Shubhojit Roy, 'Russia tells Pak: punish 26/11 perpetrators,' *Indian Express*, 22 December 2010.

14. 'Security Group Says Afghanistan Poses Threat to Central Asia,' *Radio Free Europe*, 12 March 2011, available at http://www.rferl.org/content/csto_tajikistan_afghanistan/2341893.html

15. 'Russia warns of "new wave" of terror, seeks India's help,' *Times of India*, 14 October 2012.

16. Shubhajit Roy, 'India, Russia to revive arms maintenance factory in Afghanistan,' *Indian Express*, 10 December 2013.

17. M.K. Bhadrakumar, 'Getting the regional act together,' *Hindu*, 29 August 2011.

18. K.M. Seethi, 'India's Connect Central Asia Policy,' The Diplomat, 13 December 2013.

19. Harsh V. Pant, 'A Fine Balance: India Walks a Tightrope Between Iran and the United States,' *Orbis*, Vol. 51, No. 3 (Summer 2007).

20. Harsh V. Pant, 'Delhi's Tehran Conundrum,' *Wall Street Journal*, 20 September 2010.

21. Pranab Dhal Samanta, 'Now, an India–Iran–Afghanistan tri-summit,' *Indian Express*, 21 September 2010.

22. 'India Eyes Iran Energy Sector Investment,' Press TV, 1 November 2010, http://www.presstv.ir/detail/149249.html

23. 'Iran offers oilfield, pipeline to India for raising oil import,' *Times of India*, 27 May 2013.

24. Harsh V. Pant, 'India's Relations With Iran: Much Ado About Nothing,' *Washington Quarterly*, Vol. 34, No. 1 (January 2011), 61–74.

25. Amitav Ranjan, 'As China offers funds to Iran, India set to fast-track Chabahar pact,' *Indian Express*, 1 July 2013.

26. Jayanth Jacob, 'Pakistan to give India MFN status by year end,' *Hindustan Times*, 29 February 2012.

27. Vijay C. Roy, 'New Attari post to treble India–Pak trade,' *Business Standard*, 12 April 2012.

28. Ahmad Jamal Nizami, 'China to stand by Pakistan in its hour of need: Envoy,' *Nation*, 14 July 2011.
29. Harsh V. Pant, 'The Pakistan Thorn in US–China–India Ties,' *Washington Quarterly*, Vol. 35, No. 1 (Winter 2012), 83–95.
30. Anita Joshua, 'India, Pakistan ink visa agreement,' *Hindu*, 8 September 2012.
31. 'Pak aiding infiltration: Shinde,' *Indian Express*, 22 October 2012.
32. Anita Joshua, 'JuD offers funeral prayers for Kasab,' *Hindu*, 24 November 2012.
33. Nilanjana Bhowmick, 'Kasab's Execution: After Hanging 2008 Terrorist, What Lessons Has India Learned?' *Time*, 21 November 2012.
34. Personal interview with a senior member of the National Security Council, Government of India.

REGIONAL REALITIES: AS COMPLICATED AS EVER

1. The declaration signed at the Istanbul Conference can be found at http://mfa.gov.af/en/news/4598
2. Shaida M. Abdali, 'With a little help from friends,' *Indian Express*, 10 October 2012.
3. C. Raja Mohan, 'The Essential Triangle,' *Indian Express*, 5 August 2011, http://www.indianexpress.com/news/the-essential-triangle/827305/
4. For a detailed explication of the contemporary state of Sino–Indian relations, see Harsh V. Pant, *The China Syndrome: Grappling with an Uneasy Relationship* (New Delhi: HarperCollins, 2010).
5. Ananth Krishnan, 'Behind China's India policy, a growing debate,' *Hindu*, 5 April 2010, http://www.thehindu.com/opinion/lead/article388895.ece?homepage=true
6. Ziad Haider, 'The China Factor in Pakistan,' *Far Eastern Economic Review*, 2 October 2009.
7. 'Pak now hands China a "blank cheque," India says no

way,' *Indian Express*, 23 February 2010, http://www. indianexpress.com/news/pak-now-hands-china-a-blank-cheque-india/583511/

8. Anna Fifield, 'Pakistan lets China see US helicopter,' *Financial Times*, 14 August 2011, http://www.ft.com/intl/cms/s/0/09700746-c681-11e0-bb50-00144feabdc0. html#axzz1ZwYY8g6p

9. Saibal Dasgupta, 'China mulls setting up military base in Pakistan,' *Times of India*, 28 January 2010, http://articles. timesofindia.indiatimes.com/2010-01-28/china/28120878_1_ karokoram-highway-military-bases-north-west-frontier-province

10. Selig S. Harrison, 'China's Direct Hold on Pakistan's Northern Borderlands,' *International Herald Tribune*, 26 August 2010.

11. Li Xiaokun and Li Liangxin, 'Pakistan assured of firm support,' *China Daily*, 19 May 2011, http://www.chinadaily.com.cn/ cndy/2011-05/19/content_12536794.htm

12. S.M. Burke, *Pakistan's Foreign Policy* (London: Oxford University Press, 1973), 213.

13. Tom Wright and Jeremy Page, 'China Pullout Deals Blow to Pakistan,' *Wall Street Journal*, 30 September 2011, http:// online.wsj.com/article/SB1000142405297020340550457660 0671644602028.html

14. 'China's CNPC begins oil production in Afghanistan,' Reuters, 21 October 2012.

15. Andrew Small, 'Why is China Talking to the Taliban?' *Foreign Policy*, 21 June 2013.

16. On Indian concerns about the evolving strategic situation in Afghanistan, see 'India in Afghanistan: A Test Case for a Rising Power?' *Contemporary South Asia*, Vol. 18, No. 2 (June 2010), 133–153.

17. For Pakistan's reasons in supporting Taliban and its impact on Pakistan's foreign policy, see Kenneth Weisbrode, 'Central Eurasia: Prize or Quicksand?' *Adelphi Paper 338* (London: International Institute for Strategic Studies, 2001), 68–71.

18. For a background of Iran's relations with Taliban, see Amin Saikal, 'Iran's Turbulent Neighbor: The Challenge of the Taliban,' *Global Dialogue* 3, No. 2/3 (Spring/Summer 2001): 93–103.

19. For details on the emerging contours of India–Iran relationship, see Harsh V. Pant, *Contemporary Debates in Indian Foreign and Security Policy* (New York: Palgrave Macmillan, 2008), 113–129.

20. Harsh V. Pant, 'India's Relations with Iran: Much Ado About Nothing,' *Washington Quarterly*, Vol. 34, No. 1 (January 2011), 61–74.

21. On the deteriorating security environment in Afghanistan, see Barnett R. Rubin, 'Saving Afghanistan,' *Foreign Affairs*, Vol. 86, No. 1 (January/February 2007), 57–78.

22. Atul Aneja, 'Iran: Struggling to cope with refugee crisis,' *Hindu*, 16 August 2008.

23. Kate Clark, 'Arming the Taleban,' BBC News, 18 September 2008, http://news.bbc.co.uk/2/hi/south_asia

24. David Rohde, 'Iran Is Seeking More Influence in Afghanistan,' *New York Times*, 27 December 2006.

25. John Ward Anderson, 'Arms Seized in Afghanistan Sent From Iran, NATO Says,' *Washington Post*, 21 September 2007.

26. A. Rashid, *Taliban: The Story of Afghan Warlords* (Oxford: Pan Books, 2001), 211.

27. Muhammad Tahir, 'Iranian Involvement in Afghanistan,' *Terrorism Monitor*, Vol. 5, No. 1 (January 18, 2007).

28. Luke Mogelson, 'The Scariest Little Corner of the World,' *New York Times*, 18 October 2012.

29. Sheryl Gay Stolberg, 'Bush and Karzai divided on Iran's role,' *International Herald Tribune*, 7 August 2007.

30. Nathan Hodge and Habib Khan Totakhil, 'Iran Seeks to Scuttle US Pact With Kabul,' *Wall Street Journal*, 8 May 2012.

31. Rajiv Chandrasekaran, 'Neighboring countries wary of thaw in Afghan–Pakistan relations,' *Washington Post*, 25 July 2010.

32. Walter Russell Mead, 'High Noon in Pakistan,' *American*

Interest Online, 8 May 2011.

33. Peter Beinhart, 'Why Are We in Afghanistan?' *Newsweek*, 10 June 2011.

34. Pervez Hoodboy, 'The Funambulist State,' *Outlook*, 14 May 2011.

35. Jane Perlez, 'Pakistani Army, Shaken by Raid, Faces New Scrutiny,' *New York Times*, 4 May 2011.

36. Dean Nelson, 'WikiLeaks: Pakistan Continues to Support Mumbai Terror Attack Group,' *Telegraph* (London), 1 December 2010.

37. Mukund Padmanabhan, 'State Department Cable Cited ISI Links with Militants,' *Hindu*, 31 May 2011.

38. 'JuD Holds Prayers for Osama in Lahore, Karachi,' *News* (Karachi), 4 May 2011.

39. Karen de Young, 'Pakistan Doubles Its Nuclear Arsenal,' *Washington Post*, 31 January 2011.

40. Matt Gurney, 'Pakistan Can't Be Trusted with Nuclear Weapons,' *National Post*, 2 May 2011.

41. James Lamont, 'Pakistan's Army Battles Enemy Within,' *Financial Times*, 13 June 2011.

42. Andrew Bast, 'Pakistan's Nuclear Surge,' *Newsweek*, 15 May 2011.

43. Greg Miller, 'WikiLeaks's Unveiling of Cables Shows Delicate Diplomatic Balance with Pakistan,' *Washington Post*, 28 November 2010.

44. Omar Waraich, 'WikiLeaks Shows Insecurity over Pakistan Nukes,' *Time*, 1 December 2010.

45. Rajiv Chandrasekaran, 'Former US envoy in Afghanistan Worried About Insurgent Havens in Pakistan,' *Washington Post*, 13 December 2010.

46. Karen de Young, 'Pakistan Backed Attacks on American Targets, US Says,' *Washington Post*, 23 September 2011.

47. Chidanand Rajghatta, 'US winks again at Pakistani terror tactics,' *Times of India*, 6 October 2012.

The US–India–Afghan Matrix: Confused Signals, Disastrous Consequences

1. Bob Woodward, *Obama's Wars: The Inside Story* (London: Simon & Schuster, 2010), 336.
2. Ibid.
3. C. Raja Mohan, 'Beyond US Withdrawal: India's Afghan Options,' *The American Interest*, 6 April 2012.
4. C. Raja Mohan, 'Great Game folio,' *Indian Express*, 27 January 2010.
5. Private conversation with a senior official, Ministry of Defence, Government of India, New Delhi.
6. Press Trust of India, 'Taliban praise India for resisting US pressure on Afghanistan,' 17 June 2012.
7. 'US contradicts Taliban, says India did not say no on Afghanistan,' *Indian Express*, 19 June 2012.
8. Chidanand Rajghatta, 'America persuades India to expand Afghan footprint,' *Times of India*, 14 June 2012.
9. Indrani Bagchi, 'US seal on India's key role in rebuilding Afghanistan,' *Times of India*, 20 October 2012.
10. 'US seal on India's key role in rebuilding Afghanistan,' *Times of India*, 20 October 2012.
11. These suggestions are based on the author's discussions with a number of Indian policymakers and defence officials.
12. Bob Woodward, *Obama's Wars: The Inside Story* (London: Simon & Schuster, 2010), 82–110.
13. Ibid., 302.
14. Ibid., 366.
15. Ibid., 366.
16. Khaled Ahmed, 'The pipe dream of peace,' *Indian Express*, 12 February 2014.
17. Pamela Constable, 'Afghan peace lost in transition worries,' *Washington Post*, 21 May 2013.
18. Khaled Ahmed, 'The Coming Apocalypse,' *Newsweek Pakistan*, 1 April 2014.

19. Kevin Sieff and Scott Wilson, 'Obama makes surprise trip to Afghanistan to sign key pact, mark bin Laden raid,' *Washington Post*, 2 May 2012.

20. Kevin Sieff, 'Obama's visit to Kabul opens challenging period for US–Afghan relations,' *Washington Post*, 3 May 2012.

21. Matthew Rosenberg, 'Amid Drawdown, Fears of Taliban Resurgence and Economic Collapse,' *International New York Times*, 28 May 2014.

22. Narayan Lakshman, 'Regional "anxiety" on Afghan transition: Biswal,' *Hindu*, 24 May 2014.

23. Eric Schmitt and Charlie Savage, 'Bowe Bergdahl, American Soldier, Freed by Taliban in Prisoner Trade,' *International New York Times*, 31 May 2014.

24. Matthew Rosenberg and Carlotta Gall, 'Prisoner Trade Yields Rare View Into the Taliban,' *International New York Times*, 1 June 2014.

25. Deepak Kapoor, 'Shared Stakes in Safety,' *Times of India*, 7 February 2012.

26. Pranab Dhal Samanta, 'India to pay Russia for arms, ammo it sells to Afghanistan,' *Indian Express*, 18 April 2014.

27. Kevin Sieff, 'Afghans anxious over Obama plan to end troop presence by 2016,' *Washington Post*, 28 May 2014.

28. Author's private interviews with senior Indian defence officers.

29. Vijaita Singh, 'IB told Rajnath: NATO troops withdrawal from Afghan will up infiltration, terror activities,' *Indian Express*, 16 June 2014.

30. 'After 11 years of war, al-Qaida in Afghanistan is smaller but trying to make a comeback,' *Associated Press*, 21 October 2012.

31. Qaswar Abbas, 'When US pulls out of Kabul, Delhi will have trouble in Kashmir: Hafiz Saeed,' *India Today*, 13 April 2012.

32. Praveen Swami, 'Obama's "peace at any cost" talks with Taliban may recoil on India,' *Firstpost*, 20 June 2013.

33. Jason Burke, 'Al-Qaida video urges Muslims in Kashmir to wage jihad on India,' *Guardian*, 14 June 2014.

INDEX

ACKNOWLEDGEMENTS

It was only with the help, support and encouragement of a number of people that this project could come to fruition.

This book would not have been possible without the help and guidance I have received over the years from numerous scholars, thinkers and policymakers in India who were willing to share their time and expertise with me. They talked candidly about Afghanistan, Pakistan and India's strategic environment and, in so doing, helped me better understand the complexities inherent in the making of Indian foreign policy. There is no way I can acknowledge their contributions in these few words. But my heartfelt thanks to each and every one.

Part of the book was written while I was a visiting fellow at the Observer Research Foundation (ORF), New Delhi. Thanks to Samir Saran for making this stint possible, and also to a number of young scholars who helped me as research assistants at the ORF. I also owe special thanks to Avinash Paliwal, my Ph.D student at King's College London, for all sorts of help he provided over the course of this project.

Krishan Chopra at HarperCollins India was very

enthusiastic about this project at every stage and kept me going. A number of deadlines were missed but Krishan's understanding and support never wavered. Siddhesh Inamdar did a great job of editing a manuscript that was full of loose ends to be tied. Without his careful eye, the final version of this book would have been very different.

Finally, a special note of thanks to my family—particularly my wife Tuhina, who had to put up with my long absences from home. She did so with great patience and, in so doing, considerably lightened my task.

I have dedicated this book to my daughter Vaidehi, whose contagious effervescence never ceases to be miraculous. Thank you, Vaidehi, for being a part of our lives. Here's hoping that she lives in a South Asia which is much more peaceful and stable than it has been in our lifetime.

ABOUT THE AUTHOR

Harsh V. Pant is Professor of International Relations at King's College London. He is also an associate with the King's Centre for Science and Security Studies and an affiliate with the King's India Institute. He has been a visiting professor at the Indian Institute of Management, Bangalore; a visiting fellow at the Observer Research Foundation, New Delhi; a visiting fellow at the Center for the Advanced Study of India, University of Pennsylvania; a visiting scholar at the Center for International Peace and Security Studies, McGill University; and a fellow at the Australia–India Institute, University of Melbourne. His current research is focused on Asian security issues. His recent books include *The US–India Nuclear Pact* (Oxford University Press), *The China Syndrome* (HarperCollins India), *Contemporary Debates in Indian Foreign and Security Policy* (Palgrave Macmillan) and *Indian Foreign Policy in a Unipolar World* (Routledge).